AD\
CHRISTIAN FOUN.

MW00990619

"In his latest tome, 'Christian Foundations of the Common Law', Dr Augusto Zimmermann rediscovers the Christian roots of the English, American and Australian legal systems. With scholarly acuity, this work skilfully uncovers how great thinkers in Western Civilization understood the cultural importance of these self-evident truths to society and good governance under the rule of law. At a time when perhaps we need it most, Zimmermann shows how Christian ideas like 'natural law', 'natural rights' and 'natural justice', contributed to the development of the common law. In doing so, Dr Zimmermann's work convincingly confirms for us that ideas informed by the Bible influenced in important ways the development of the Common Law, and indeed, the preservation of freedom and justice. Woven through the very readable chapters of this book is a profound understanding of an ancient sacred premise: God revealed moral absolutes in His Word, and placed these truths on the human heart".

William Wagner, Distinguished Professor Emeritus of Law, Western Michigan University, U.S.A., Former U.S. Federal Judge & U.S. Diplomat, President, Salt & Light Global

"Professor Zimmermann's book is striking in its depth and breadth. Not since Harold Berman's volumes on Law and Revolution has such a mammoth task been undertaken. Berman's positive influence is clear in the way Zimmermann systematically and incontrovertibly demonstrates the Christian roots of the common law in Australia, England and the US. Yet Zimmermann goes further than Berman in at least two respects. First, he delves deeply into three particular jurisdictions and focuses on influential political figures in an enlightening way. Second, Zimmermann skilfully takes into account recent developments in Western politics and culture and a broad range of contemporary scholarship in theology, legal theory and history, philosophy and constitutional law. This book is therefore informative for scholars and laity alike, and essential reading for a legal community which seems content to drift ever further from its Christian origins. I highly recommend it."

Dr Alex Deagon FHEA, Senior Lecturer in Law, Queensland University of Technology, Author of 'From Violence to Peace: Theology, Law and Community'

"Professor Augusto Zimmermann has produced an extremely helpful book in which he carefully demonstrates the indissociable Christian origins of the common law. This is a most timely publication, particularly in the context of contemporary discourse that attempts to relativise religious influence. Professor Zimmermann traces how many of our current freedoms within a broad, plural, public square can be attributed to a rich seam of Christian philosophical influence that has evidently infused the development of the common law in different jurisdictions. In my view, this is essential reading for students and scholars alike who seek a fuller appreciation as to the origins of the common law."

Simon McCrossan LL.M, Barrister, UK, Head of Public Policy, Evangelical Alliance UK

"If we forget our history we are destined to repeat mistakes of the past. If we are not truthful about our history we cannot understand our present. It is popular today to attempt to whitewash the positive influence of religion not only from the present but also from the past. The idea that law is morally neutral and that religion generally and Christianity in particular is a force of evil and not good has become popular in Australia's mainstream press and embraced by politicians and academics. In this excellent book Dr Zimmermann carefully lays out for the reader an easily digestible and highly readable account of the Christian roots of the common law in England, the United States and Australia. His book is a very valuable addition to Australian works on legal history and will assist not only lawyers and law students but all interested readers to better understand why our legal system is as it is. The work also provides an understanding of the dangers of forgetting the common laws roots in Christianity and in particular in the use of reason grounded in faith. It demands publication".

Michael Quinlan, Dean & Professor of Law, The University of Notre Dame Australia, (Sydney)

"I very much enjoyed reading this book by Dr Augusto Zimmermann. I think the book has the great potential to have a timeless impact and its historical overview of the Christian foundations of the common law and the laws of the U.S. and Australia is thorough, important and timely. In sum, this is an excellent and timely work, for which I deeply commend its author".

Michael V. Hernandez, Dean & Professor of Law, Regent University School of Law, U.S.A.

"In an age of cynicism, apathy and despair Professor Zimmermann's book comes as a fresh and timely reminder to not neglect the legal and parliamentary Christian foundations of our nation. With well researched material, this book documents how the history of Common Law is intrinsically intertwined with the Christian faith. It is a very enlightening, inspiring and encouraging contribution, documenting this important aspect of Australia's Christian heritage. Every Australian needs to read it to appreciate our heritage of freedom, which one hundred thousand Australians sacrificed their lives to defend in two world wars".

Dr Graham McLennan, Chairman, National Alliance of Christian Leaders (NACL), Joint Founder, Christian History Research website (www.chr.org.au)

"From the perspective of a practitioner whose daily routine is arguing in court, Augusto Zimmermann's Christian Foundations of the Common Law, with its encyclopaedic English, American and Australian perspective, is an elegant commentary on the relation between the law and ideas, both theological and philosophical. The part devoted to the United States is particularly significant for the rest of the common law world whose law is so much influenced by that country. This is a must read book for anyone who wishes to understand where we are and where we came from."

Michael McAuley, President, St Thomas More Society (Australia), Barrister, Selborne Chambers (Sydney)

"We are indebted to Augusto Zimmermann for his magnificent account of the role played by Christian philosophy in the development of the legal systems of England, the U.S. and Australia. This is a highly significant and original work, written with great clarity and directness yet displaying profound historical and theological scholarship. It is especially relevant in our times when scant attention is paid to the contribution of Christian values and beliefs to human life. This book will enrich the understanding of many, but it will also challenge and irritate that realm of secularist thought that sees Christianity as a dark and sinister presence on the human condition"

Michael Mc Mahon OMI, Department of Religious Education and English, Mazenod College, Perth

"Professor Zimmermann's book is outstanding in its breadth and depth. The Christian influence on the legal institutions that have come to define the West is proven beyond doubt in this work. Zimmermann's study brings together not just the best historical, legal, and philosophical analyses on the question of the origins and evolution of the West's legal traditions, but also offers original insights of its own. More and more, in spite of the declarations of secularist triumphalists, we are discovering that the institutions that have brought so much freedom and stability to the West are indeed a result of a complex set of historical traditions and practices evolving in dialogue with Christian institutions and ideas. If it is perilous for a civilization to forget the traditions that have nourished and animated its most successful and valuable institutions, then Zimmermann's book is not merely a fascinating read but also indispensable for the task of preserving modern liberties against various creeping totalitarianisms, secularist and religious."

Dr Stephen Chavura B.A. (Hons. I), Ph.D. (UNE), Senior Research Associate, Department of Modern History and Politics, Macquarie University, Sydney.

"At a time when Christianity is being pushed out of the public square, Dr Zimmermann's latest book is a timely and important antidote to the modern myth that our common law rights emerged from thin air or was a gift from international bodies like the United Nations. In fact, as Dr Zimmermann's historical analysis reveals, the reason we have a public square is because of early English legal developments driven by theologians and Christian jurists. Dr Zimmermann has yet again made an important contribution to the legal literature which should be required reading by all first year law students (as well as the lecturers!)".

Morgan Begg, Research Fellow, Institute of Public Affairs (Melbourne)

"Christianity, history and law all get a bad rap nowadays. They are ignored, denounced or misrepresented. Yet all three are vital to modern democracies, and all three are closely related as Dr Zimmerman so brilliantly demonstrates in this important volume. This exceedingly thorough, well-researched, and well-written book is essential reading for those who would see faith and freedom retain their much-needed role in Western society".

Bill Muehlenberg, CultureWatch, Author of *'Modern Conservative Thought'*

Christian Foundations of the Common Law

Volume 2

The United States

Augusto Zimmermann

Connor Court Publishing

First published in 2018 by Connor Court Publishing Pty Ltd

ISBN: 9781925826067

Connor Court Publishing Pty Ltd
Suite 2, 146 Boundary Street
West End, Queensland, Australia, 4101
sales@connorcourt.com
www.connorcourtpublishing.com.au

Phone 0497 900 685

Front Cover Picture: Howard Chandler Christy's Scene at the Signing of the Constitution of the United States, Wikipedia Commons.

Cover design: Maria Giordano

"The Christian religion, which ordains that men should love each other, would without doubt have every nation blest with the best civil, the best political laws; because these, next to this religion, are the greatest good that men can give and receive".

Charles-Louis de Secondat (Baron de Montesquieu) *The Spirit of Laws* (1748) Bk XXIV, Ch 1

CONTENTS

Preface

In 2013 Professor Augusto Zimmermann published *Western Legal Theory: History, Concepts and Perspectives* in which he described and analysed most legal theories which contributed to the development of the Common Law. Now he has published a highly readable account of the Christian roots of the Common Law legal systems of England, the United States and Australia. As such, *Christian Foundations of the Common Law* beautifully complements his earlier book. Together, these books constitute remarkably significant contributions to Legal History, Legal Theory and the Common Law.

Professor Zimmermann is a very influential Australian who has taught at a number of universities worldwide and has served as a Law Reform Commissioner in Western Australia. He is the President of the Western Australian Legal Theory Association (WALTA) as well as the Editor-in-Chief of the *Western Australian Jurist*, which has published a plethora of excellent articles on the Christian roots of the Common Law.

I am delighted to write the Foreword to *Christian Foundations of the Common Law*. My delight stems from the fact that the book is a lucid description of the roots of the Common Law as well as a persuasive and cogent analysis of the role of religion in modern society.

In 2004 I published an article entitled *The Menace of Neutrality in Religion* in the Brigham Young University Law Review (Volume 2004, Number 2, pp. 535-574). The article deals essentially with the conflict between religion, on the one hand, and the demands and expectations of our secular world, on the other. In particular, it concerns the role that religion and religious discourse are able to play in the public forum. In the article I noted that church attendance has substantially collapsed in most Western countries. In addition, many leaders of established religions are no longer able (or willing) to serve as moral standard bearers. Indeed, even a perfunctory review of the state of religion in Western societies reveals that organised religions are in turmoil which, at least in part, is a consequence of the seeming inability (or unwillingness) of the leaders of organised religions to support the moral foundations and tenets of their own faith. Now, 14 years later, the situation described in 2004 has only exacerbated as is evidenced by the public investigations into child sexual abuse committed by priests and the revelations made in the Royal Commission into Institutional Responses to Child Sexual Abuse in Australia (and similar enquiries in a number of other countries as well). There is no doubt that organised religions (or 'churches') have lost their erstwhile authority and moral supremacy in an increasingly secular world.

What should be the appropriate response to the obvious decline of organised religions and the associated crisis of faith? In my opinion, the response should not be to abandon religion, but to maintain the faith upon which one's religion is based. This is because most of the criticism directed at organised religions confounds 'church' and 'religion' and erroneously uses these two nouns interchangeably. But the misbehaviour of some leaders of established religions (or 'churches') should not be used as a reason for abandoning religion and for denigrating the valuable role that religion continues to make to the maintenance of a decent and civilised society under the rule of law. Indeed, it is perfectly possible to condemn the egregious attitudes and behaviours of church leaders and individual adherents of a religion, whilst at the same time champion and nurture the role that religious faith plays in society and in individuals' lives. Whereas an organised religion (or 'church') is predominantly a collection of people who profess the same faith, religion is an intensively personal activity even if it is exercised in community with others. Religion involves the relationship between individuals and a Supreme Being. Hence, it is entirely possible for a person to be anti-church or anti-established religions but still be religious and spiritual.

Another consequence of the palpable decline in the moral authority of established religions (or 'churches') is that religious discourse is often seen as divisive and unsuitable for rational discussion in the public forum. Increasingly, religion discourse is no longer seen as able to make constructive contributions to the discussion of the topical issues of our times. Hence, issues such as same-sex marriage, euthanasia, gender choice, biological experiments, even the effect of the implementation of section 18C of the *Racial Discrimination Act* 1974 (Cth) on free speech, among others, exclude religious viewpoints because they are viewed as discriminatory, unenlightened, uninformed, biased and arcane.

It is fair to say that in Australia, Catholic Schools (or perhaps 'Christian' schools more generally) are probably the only educational institutions where genuine dialogue about various cultural views/opinions is still tolerated. This tolerance stems from the identifiable characteristics of a Catholic (or Christian)

School: a diverse educational climate, personal development of students, focus on the relationship between the Gospel and human culture, and an examination of knowledge in the light of faith. Such a dialogue is hardly possible in public educational institutions, including universities, because these institutions aggressively and routinely promote secular ideologies as the only acceptable views. Sadly, any challenge to secular ideologies are met with conniptions, outrage, scepticism and ridicule. This is compounded by the fact that religious viewpoints are usually treated with contempt and sustained hostility in the media.

These are tragic developments because, in entrenching a secular society which is devoid of religious viewpoints, we are losing the knowledge of, and appreciation for, the close relationship between our Christian heritage and the development of the Common Law.

Christian Foundations of the Common Law is therefore a timely reminder of the close link between Christianity and the Common Law. It reminds us that our democracy and great institutions are shaped by, and inspired by, and are certainly based on Christianity – a fact that is often conveniently overlooked by scholars and lawyers. This book represents a veritable *tour de force* because it meticulously describes the influence of the Christian heritage on the development of our Common Law legal system. It particularly well describes and traces the Christian origins of the Common Law legal system in England, the United States and Australia.

The Christian heritage of the Common Law is not often discussed in the law schools of the three jurisdictions chosen by Professor Zimmermann. Even if such a discussion does find its way into the curriculum, the topic is treated as a mere by-

16

product of issues which are considered to be more important and amenable to rational discussion. Professor Zimmermann's book is likely to remind our law teachers, politicians and trend-setters of the importance of Christianity to the development of the Common Law. Hopefully, in emphasising the Christian roots of the main Common Law legal systems, we will be able to rejuvenate the curriculum in Australian, English and American law schools. For example, there can be little doubt that natural law, natural rights, the Magna Carta and Canon Law have positively impacted the development of, and have commanded respect for, the rule of law in Common Law jurisdictions.

In all three jurisdictions, discussed by Professor Zimmermann, the Christian faith is still acknowledged in a symbolic way in ceremonies, such as the ceremonial opening of Parliament or at the start of the judicial year. Even in the United States, although the First Amendment to the American Constitution has been interpreted as requiring the separation of church and state – a most controversial and litigious constitutional principle – the influence of religion on public life is still evident. In any event, the separation of church and state principle is not meant to discriminate against religion, but instead, as Roger Williams argued in the 18th century, to protect religion from the state. Williams addressed these issues in his eloquent metaphor of the wilderness and the garden. For Williams, the garden was the place of God's people, those of faith; outside the garden was the un-evangelised world of the wilderness, requiring the construction of a hedge to separate the two worlds and to protect religion from the state.

This book is a timely, relevant and important contribution to an understanding of the Christian origins of the Australian,

English and American legal systems. As such, it is not only an admirable example of Legal History at its best, but also a philosophical treatise that questions, challenges and guides its readers.

This is an eminently readable book which should be read by law students, legal academics, practising lawyers and the judiciary. I also recommend the book to those who, although they may not have been trained in the rigorous discussion of legal and moral issues, are nevertheless interested in understanding the legal, philosophical and Christian roots of our legal system.

Hence, it is with pleasure that I recommend this book to the widest possible readership. This book is erudite, informative, well-written and researched and most importantly, it is a timely reminder of the Christian heritage of the Common Law that has served us so well for many centuries.

Gabriël A. Moens
Emeritus Professor of Law, The University of Queensland
Professor of Law, Curtin University

ACKNOWLEDGEMENTS

Writing three volumes about the Christian foundations of the common law is a deeply challenging task.

In the more crucial phases of manuscript preparation, I was assisted by an outstanding law student of mine, Mr Bruce Linkermann. In the final phase, I was assisted by another outstanding law student of mine, Mr Heath Harley-Bellemore.

Both Bruce and Heath are now graduated. They are extraordinary young lawyers in Western Australia. Above all, I am very blessed to call them my special friends.

I also would like to acknowledge the assistance of another friend, Mr Joshua Forrester. He is an outstanding legal philosopher, currently undertaking PhD research under my supervision. I am thankful to him for his constructive feedback and for telling me when any aspect of the work needed further improvement.

Also, I would like to thank Emeritus Professor Gabriël A. Moens for writing the preface to these volumes. Professor Moens is a leading legal academic in Australia and I have a profound admiration for him.

To all these wonderful friends I can only express my deepest gratitude.

Of course, I am solely responsible for the text and hence any omissions are entirely my fault. In a work of this magnitude there are bound to be a couple of errors. I can only hope they are not so many.

Finally, Anthony Cappello, the competent editor of Connor

Court Publishing, provided crucial advice in the editing of the final manuscripts.

It is my sincerest hope that the reader of these volumes enjoy the experience as much as I deeply enjoyed writing them!

The present work is wholeheartedly dedicated to Bruna, Elizabeth and Gabriel.

SOLI DEO GLORIA.

– **Professor Augusto Zimmermann**, Sheridan College, WA - March 2018

'By the Providence of Almighty God':

Christian Foundations of the American Legal System

'Our Constitution was made only for a moral and religious people. It is wholly inadequate to the government of any other'.
– John Adams (1798)[1]

'America was born a Christian nation. America was born to exemplify that devotion to the elements of righteousness which are derived from the revelations of Holy Scripture.'
– President Woodrow Wilson (1911)[2]

---

[1]   Message from John Adams to the Officers of the First Brigade, October 11, 1798, available at http://www.beliefnet.com/resourcelib/docs/115/Message_from_John_Adams_to_the_Officers_of_the_First_Brigade_1.html

[2]   Arthur S. Link (ed.), *The Papers of Woodrow Wilson* - 57 volumes (Princeton/NJ: Princeton University Press, 1966), 23:12-20.

21

13

'By the Providence of Almighty God' - First Considerations

The United States of America inherited many aspects of the English law, including its rich Christian heritage. Christianity was central to the lives of the New World colonists and their faith dominated their society and formed the foundations of their legal traditions. Leading up to the American Revolution, and continuing thereafter, American society evolved and largely departed from its English foundations. Primarily, the American Revolution was fuelled by ideals and principles which were overtly Christian. This is reflected in the fact that numerous American Founders – Benjamin Franklin, John Adams, and George Washington (to name just a few) – drew heavily from their Christian faith when laying the foundations for their country. George Washington, for example, considered that 'it is the duty of all nations to acknowledge the providence of Almighty God, to obey His will, to be grateful for His benefits, and humbly to implore His protection and favor'.[3] Washington went on to state in his Thanksgiving Proclamation of October

---

3   James D. Richardson, *A Compilation of the Messages and Papers of the Presidents, 1789-1897*, vol. I (Washington/DC: Bureau of National Literature and Art, 1901)

3rd, 1789, that, as a nation, 'we [i.e., Americans] may then unite in most humbly offering our prayers and supplications to the great Lord and Ruler of Nations, and beseech Him to pardon our national and other transgressions'.[4]

Published in two volumes, the first in 1835 and the second in 1840, Alexis de Tocqueville's *Democracy in America* is a seminal work that examines the pivotal role of Christianity in the formation of the United States. After recognising that the nation's Founders intended it to be a Christian nation, it views the relationship between Christianity and American law and society as central to a more proper understanding of the moral requirements of freedom and the proper tasks of democratic government. 'The Americans combine the notions of Christianity and of liberty so intimately in their minds, that it is impossible to make them conceive the one without the other', Tocqueville wrote.[5] The intrinsic correlation between Christianity and American law and political institutions is explained as follows:

> But there is no country in the world where the Christian religion retains a great influence over the souls of men than in America; and there can be no greater proof of its utility, and of its conformity to human nature, than that its influence is powerfully felt over the most enlightened and free nation of the earth [...] Religion in America [...] must be regarded as the first of their political institutions; for if it does not impart a taste for freedom, it facilitates the use of it [...] I don't know whether all the Americans have a sincere faith in their religion – for how can search the human heart? But I am certain that they hold it to indispensable to

4   Ibid.
5   Alexis De Tocqueville, *Democracy in America* (New York/NY: Barnes & Noble, 2003), p 258.

the maintenance of republican institutions. This opinion is not peculiar to a class of citizens, or to a party, but it belongs to the whole nation and to every rank of society.[6]

Christianity formed the character of American society from the very beginning. The principles of Christianity lie at the heart of the American experiment. Such principles derive from 'Christian convictions as to how we should conduct our lives, how we should treat our [fellow] human beings, and what makes life worth living'.[7] As advocated by the American Founders, these principles assert the supremacy of the elected legislature coupled with judicial independence from political pressure and the reliance of judges on institutional arrangements aiming to protect 'natural rights' of the individual, and establish 'government under the law'. Accordingly, such rights impose constitutional limits on the government, working as a prescription for a system of checks and balances whereby the exercise of power is limited by a citizens' right to not be subjected to unjust laws.[8] This provides a rational basis on which citizens can affirm institutional limits to what their government can do. As noted by Russell Kirk,

> Natural rights and duties all are part of a divine plan for human destiny. They are the laws and rights and duties that arise from the enduring nature that God has given to human beings. The Christian believes that human nature does not change: the character of man in this world always will be what is now, to the end of tie – a mixture of good and evil. Therefore these natural rights and duties always will endure. It is better for a man to die than to surrender

---

[6] Ibid, p 257.
[7] Russell Kirk, *The American Cause* (Wilmington/DE: ISI Books, 2002 p 30
[8] Charles Rice, *50 Questions on the Natural Law: What It Is and Why We Need It* (San Francisco/CA: Ignatius Press, 1999), p 85.

25

his natural rights to ignore his natural duties. And this Christian concept of right and duties lie at the foundation of American society and government.[9]

---

[9]   Kirk, above n.7, p 27.

14

Christianity and Law in Colonial America

In order to set the stage for a broader analysis of the Christian foundations and underpinnings of the American legal system, it is necessary to observe first the English heritage that the colonies in the "New World" inherited. Throughout the sixteenth and seventeenth centuries, French, Spanish, Dutch and English colonisation of North America displaced the traditional indigenous laws and customs of the Native Americans. As England began to expand their colonisation of the sub-continent, the other European colonies began to recede, leaving that northern region of the "New World" predominantly for the English.[10]

The English colonies in North America did not write their laws and did not establish their political institutions on a blank slate. In those days the reach of Christianity extended far beyond the realm of personal faith; it influenced, and in many cases deeply transformed, the entire socio-political landscape. As the master historian in Puritan studies, Perry Miller points out, 'without some understanding of Puritanism ... there is no understanding of America'.[11] He was basically acknowledging

---

[10] Lawrence M Friedman, *American Law* (New York/NY: Norton, 1984), p 37.
[11] Perry Miller and Thomas H. Johnson (eds.), *The Puritans* (New York/NY: American Book Co., 1938), p 1.

that Puritan ideas were deeply embedded in early American society, affecting the behaviour of the early settlers and their posterity for decades to come. The Puritans (i.e., English Calvinists) believed in 'covenant theology', meaning that God establishes covenants with his 'elected people' throughout the ages.[12] Accordingly, they thought that governments should be established by means of a 'social contract'; that is, through a covenant between the governing and the governed. This variety of Calvinism, writes Mark A. Noll,

> held that the basis for individual salvation was God's covenant-promise that he would redeem those who placed their trust in Christ. Puritans explained that promise as the outworking of a covenant within the Godhead whereby the Father chose those who would be saved, the Son accomplished their redemption, and the Spirit made it effective.[13]

In 17th-century England life was made especially difficult for the Puritans and other Non-conformists who were not members of the government-established Church of England.[14] So they began to look for other areas where they could migrate

---

12 Mark A. Noll, 'British and French North America to 1765', *in* Stewart J. Brown and Timothy Tackett (eds.), *Christianity: Enlightenment, Reawakening and Revolution 1660-1815* (Cambridge University Press, 2006), p 394.
13 Ibid., p 398.
14 'In 1625, Charles I took the throne, and also took to himself a Roman Catholic queen; worse still, he showed marked favouritism to a new party in the church which was both 'Arminian' and dogmatically 'prelatical'. Charles made the leader of that party, Bishop William Laud of London, one of his most trusted advisers, and in 1633 appointed him archbishop of Canterbury. Coupled with the king's high-handed dealings with Parliament and his weak foreign policy in the face of the growing power of Roman Catholic France, these polices began to dim Puritan hops for England's Future. As a consequence, the more dogmatic and especially the more congregationally inclined among them began in ever larger numbers to despair of root and branch reform. Singly or in groups some fled to Holland. Then, during the decade of the 1630s, the great Puritan migration to America took place'. – Sydney E. Ahlstrom, *A Religious History of the American People* (New Haven/CT: Yale University Press, 1927), p 93.

28

to freely exercise their Christian faith.[15] Although Puritan theology held that the Kingdom of Christ not just could but it most positively would be advanced on earth, the Puritans were people under intense persecution in England. They were being constantly imprisoned, hanged, or burned at the stake. Their properties were often seized, and government agents watched them relentlessly.[16]

Despite all these trials Puritan theology was by no means escapist. On the contrary, as its core such a theology was profoundly hopeful. It expected a final victory in its peaceful conquering work for Christ. Above all, the Puritans were convinced of God's ultimate victory over the forces of evil and darkness operating in the world. So convinced were they of Christ's final victory that even when they were chased out of England ("harried from the land" as King James I termed it), still they looked forward in the expectation of advancing Christ's kingdom on a remote continent.[17] Rod Gragg explains this fundamental element of early American colonization:

> Covenant theology and the Puritan desire to 'purify' the Church of England – the official government denomination – were not popular with English monarchs. Neither was the Puritan belief that all people were equal before God. King James I vowed to 'harry them out of the land, or else do worse', and his son and successor, King Charles I, permitted Anglican officials to persecute them. Puritan preaching was restricted, their books and tracts were banned, and many Puritans were whipped, tortured,

[15] Paul Johnson, *A History of the American People* (New York/NY: Harper Perennial, 1999), p 22.
[16] Ibid., p 51.
[17] John Bona and Don Schanzenbach, *The Liberty Book: How Freedom Can & Will be Won* (Racine/WI: Broadstreet, 2016), pp 51-2.

branded, or imprisoned. Facing increased persecution, scores of Puritans prayerfully chose to follow the Pilgrims to America. Between 1630 to 1640 – in what became known as the Great Migration – more than twenty thousand Puritans immigrated to Massachusetts Bay Colony, bringing with them the seeds of Bible-based liberty.[18]

The English presence in the 'New Continent' began at the Jamestown settlement in the early 17th century. To those who ran the Virginia Company from London, the settlement's goal was 'to preach and baptise into the Christian Religion and by propagation of the Gospell, to recover out of the arms of the Devill, a number of poure and miserable soules, wrapt up into death, in almost invincible ignorance.'[19] As can be seen, the colonisation of Virginia had a distinctly Puritan or Calvinist tone. Enacted in 1606, the colony's first charter reveals the 'humble and well-intended desires' of the settlers to, 'by providence of Almighty God … propagate the Christian religion to such people, as yet live in darkness and miserable ignorance of the true knowledge and worship of God.'[20] Those settlers in Virginia were committed to the establishment of a Christian commonwealth. Their deepest desire was to remake the world in conformity with God's laws as they understood them.

Under the leadership of Lord De La Ware (or Delaware as the settlers wrote it), America's first legal code was enacted in Virginia, in 1611. It stated the colony's faithful reliance on the 'Lawes Divine, Moral and Martiall'. This legal code declared

---

18 Rod Gragg, *By the Hand of Providence: How Faith Shaped the American Revolution* (New York/NY: Howard Books, 2012), p 13.

19 Quoted in Johnson, above n.15, p 23.

20 The First Charter of Virginia (1606), in William Waller Hening (ed), *The Statutes at Large: Being a Collection of all the Laws of Virginia, From the First Session of the Legislature, in the Year 1619* (Richmond/VA: J & G Cochran, 1821), p 58.

also the Holy Bible as the primary foundation for Virginia's 'Articles, Laws, and Orders' (1610-1611).[21] In that same year, the first measure of Virginia's House of Burgesses (America's first legislative assembly) was to open its Inaugural Session with a Christian prayer and to enact a legislative requirement urging all the colonial inhabitants to attend church service on Sundays (the 'Lord's Day'). Two days later, the first Constitution of Virginia was enacted with its Preamble dedicating the colony to 'To the Advancement of the Honour and Service of God, and the Enlargement of His Kingdom.'[22]

The second permanent English colony established in North America was New Plymouth, in December 1620. Soon the colony started to be known Massachusetts. Sixteen years after its foundation, its General Court enacted the first legal code of Massachusetts. Such a code emphasises biblical principles and it declared rules that are 'agreeable to the word of God'.[23] The first settlers in Massachusetts were distinguished for their strong Calvinist beliefs which made them particularly unwilling to submit to the 'false teachings' of the Church of England. They were called 'Puritans' due to their desire to 'purify' that established church of what they thought to be unbiblical doctrines and practices. As they migrated to America those Puritans sought a new kind of 'Holy Commonwealth', which would be entirely countercultural in the ardent desire to provoke 'a revolution of the saints'.[24] In other words, they had

[21] Daniel L. Dreisbach and Mark David Hall, 'Introduction', in Daniel L. Dreisbach and Mark David Hall (eds.), Faith and the Founders of the American Republic (New York/NY: Oxford University Press, 2014), p 1.
[22] Gragg, above n.18, p 10.
[23] John Eidsmoe, Christianity and the Constitution: The Faith of our Founding Fathers (Grand Rapids/MI: Baker Books, 1987), p 33.
[24] Ahlstrom, above n.14, p 129.

migrated to America in the hope to pursue not only religious freedom, but also to establish a 'Holy Commonwealth' based on biblical values and principles. As Noll points out,

> The effort by Puritans to create a purer Christian civilization than they had known in England represented North America's most comprehensive and influential religious experiment. The English Puritans, who attempted in old England to reform the lives of individuals, the practice of the national English church, and the structures of their society, were frustrated first by royal opposition and then by the ambiguities of their own temporary success in the Civil War. In the new world, by contrast, Puritan colonists were able actually to implement the principles for which they had long struggled.[25]

Since the primary motivation of those Puritans was to establish a 'Holy Commonwealth' in the 'New Continent', prior to going ashore at Plymouth, on 21 November 1620, they assembled in the cabin of their ship to devise a social compact which provided for 'just and equal laws' steeped in biblical principles, in particular the Old Testament covenant between God and the 'chosen people'. The drafters of this 'new covenant' called it the 'Mayflower Compact'. They understood it to form a contract which aimed at securing unity and providing for a Christian community in 'New England'. The document's opening lines states: 'In the name of God, Amen. We whose names are underwritten ... by the grace of God ... having undertaken, for the glory of God, and advancement of the Christian faith ...'.[26] As noted by Paul Johnson,

> what was remarkable about this particular contract was

---

[25] Noll, above n.12, p 397.
[26] Ibid.

that it was not between a servant and a master, or a people and a king, but between a group of like-minded individuals and each other, with God as a witness and symbolic co-signatory.[27]

While colonial law seemed to comply with the English law in numerous respects, the colonists developed unique laws applicable to their peculiar situation and particular beliefs. Some of these legal codes quoted entire sections of the Bible. A favourite passage among the colonialists is found in Isaiah 33:22: 'The Lord is our Judge, the Lord is our Law-giver, the Lord is our King – The Lord will save us.'[28] The evidence that Christian morality was the foundation of the law and culture in early American colonial history is revealed, inter alia, in the opening statement to the 1643 *Articles of Confederation of the United Colonies of New England*:

> Whereas we all came into these parts of America with one and the same end and aim, namely, to advance the Kingdom of our Lord Jesus Christ and to enjoy the liberties of the Gospel in purity with peace ...[29]

John Winthrop (1587-1649) was an English Puritan lawyer and one of the leading figures in founding the Massachusetts Bay Colony, the second major settlement in New England, following Plymouth. He was the first influential leader to emerge in the 'New Continent'. Winthrop aspired to establish a 'godly community' based on a system of government that should function according to 'Christ's teachings'. In 1630, on the deck of the Arbella and halfway between England and Cape Cod, Winthrop persuaded his fellow-voyagers to make a solemn

---

[27] Johnson, above n.15, p 30.
[28] Ibid.
[29] Gragg, above n.18, p 3.

pact, or sacred covenant, with the God of Israel. He highlighted the global importance of the entire colonial experiment as follows:

> The Lord will be our God and delight to dwell among us, as His own people, and will command a blessing upon us in all our ways, so that we shall see much more of His wisdom, power, goodness, and truth than formerly we have been acquainted with. We shall find that the God of Israel is among us, when ten of us shall be able to resist a thousand of our enemies, when He shall make us a praise and glory, that men shall say of succeeding plantation, 'The Lord make it like that of New England'. For we must consider that we shall be as a city upon a hill, the eyes of all people are upon us.[30]

Under Winthrop's competent leadership, the settlers in New England set about establishing a community embedded with strong biblical symbolism. He headed an elected government comprised of citizens who were selected on the basis of 'Godly behaviour'. As noted by Johnson,

> He regarded himself as a man chosen by God and the people to create a new civil society from nothing by the light of his religious beliefs, and he prayed earnestly to discharge this mandate virtuously. He admitted his shortcomings, at any rate to himself. His political theory was clear. Man had liberty not to do what he liked – that was for the beasts – but to distinguish between good and evil by studying God's commands, and then to do 'that only which is good'. If, by God's grace, you were given this liberty, you had a corresponding duty to obey divinely sanctioned authority. In the blessed colony of

---

[30] John Winthrop, 'A Model of Christian Charity', *in* Perry Miller (ed.), *The American Puritans: Their Prose and Poetry* (New York: Doubleday, 1956), p 78-83.

Massachusetts, freeman chose their rulers. But, once chosen, the magistrate's world must be obeyed – it was divine law as well as man's ... Winthrop could claim that he was freely elected governor of the colony, not just once but four times, and that therefore he embodied representative government.[31]

Next to Winthrop, the second most influential leader in early colonial history was a Londoner of Welsh descent called Roger Williams (1603-1683). Ordained a Christian minister in 1628, Williams migrated to the Bay Colony in 1631, and soon started to deeply empathise with the American Indians. Although he believed in everyone's right to preserve one's conscience guided by the inner light of his particular faith, Williams none the less resented that the New Englanders apparently weren't making enough efforts to instruct the Indians in the light of the Gospels.

When Williams was forced out of the colony because of his controversial views, he went on to establish a new settlement on a site named Providence. There he sought to establish a free society based on the ideals of religious freedom and tolerance. Soon to be renamed 'Rhode Island and Providence Plantations',[32] the preamble of his colony's instrument of government stated: 'The form of government established in Providence Plantations is democratical, that is to say, a government held by the free and voluntary consent of all, or the greater part of the free

---

[31] Johnson, above n.15, pp 45-6.
[32] 'Basic to Williams's approach is the protection of individual rights, including most prominently individual (and minority) rights of conscience. However important the people's will may be, whether expressed unanimously or by majority rule, a legitimate government – one not deprived of 'natural freedom by the power of tyrants' – has an irreducible obligation to safeguard 'any civil right or privilege' due a citizen simply as a human being... or what he calls in another place the 'natural and civil rights and liberties' of all citizens'. – David Little, *Essays on Religion and Human Rights* (Cambridge University Press, 2015), p 265.

inhabitants.' Such a document closes with a ringing manifesto declaring Rhode Island to be a 'Holy Commonwealth':

> These are the laws that concern all men, and these are the penalties for the transgressions thereof, which, by common consent, are ratified and established throughout the whole Colony. And otherwise than thus, what is herein forbidden, all men may walk as their consciences persuade them, everyone in the name of his God. And let the saints of the Most High walk in this Colony without molestation, in the name of Jehovah their God, for ever and ever.[33]

The settlement in Rhode Island warmly welcomed dissidents from all Christian denominations. The colony was soon to become a great shelter for all those who were distressed and persecuted for conscience's sake. Indeed, it did not take so long for Rhode Island to acquire the reputation of being the greatest refuge for people of all religious persuasions. It also became a place where the American Indians were honoured and protected.[34] According to Johnson:

> Rhode Island was ... the first colony to make complete freedom of religion, as opposed to a mere degree of toleration, the principle of its existence, and to give this as a reason for separating church and state. Its existence of course opened the doors to the more singular sects, such as the Quakers and the Baptists, and indeed to missionaries from the Congregationalists of the Bay Colony and the Anglicans of Virginia ... The creation of Rhode Island was thus a critical turning point-point in the evolution of America. It not only introduced the principles of complete religious freedom and the separation of church and state,

---

[33] Ahlstrom, above n.14, p 168.
[34] Johnson, above n.15, p 49.

it also inaugurated the practice of religious competition ...
Rhode Island was ... in existence to provide a competitive
field in which the religious – or at any rate the varieties of
Christianity – could grapple at will, the first manifestation
of that competitive spirit which was to blow mightily over
every aspect of American existence.[35]

Another remarkable leader in early American history is
undoubtedly William Penn (1644–1718). He was not only the
founder of the Province of Pennsylvania, in 1682, but also an
entrepreneur and a committed Quaker. Like all the Quakers,
Penn was in the vanguard of the forces of change. He believed
that a basic requirement for a good society is to be governed
by 'godly rulers'.[36] 'If thou wouldst rule well, thou must rule
for God, and to do that, thou must be ruled by him ...Those
who will not be governed by God will be ruled by tyrants',
Penn wrote. In his *First Frame of Government* (Pennsylvania's
first written constitution), it is explicitly manifested that since
both government and religion ultimately derive from 'the same
divine power', then the civil government is 'a part of religion
itself, a thing sacred in its institution and end'.[37] The Christian
principles that Penn set forth would serve as an inspiration for
the concept of limited government under the law, which later
served as an inspiration for the U.S. Constitution. In the 1660s
and 1670s, writes David Little,

> Penn formed strong Whig affiliations, agreeing with them
> on the importance of limited government based on the rule
> of law and consent of the governed. Fundamental English

[35] Ibid, p 51.
[36] Cited in David Little, 'Constitutional Protection of the Freedom of Conscience in Colonial America', *in* Timothy Samuel Shah and Allan D. Hertzke (eds.), *Christianity and Freedom – Volume I: Historical Perspectives* (Cambridge University Press, 2016), p 248
[37] Ibid.

law, which for Penn embodied that tradition, rested on both theological-rational and historical premises. As were all governments, it was subject to the principle of 'Synteresis' or 'Universal Reason', a combination of divine and natural law.[38]

As can be seen, the early roots of today's American society are found in the principles of Christianity. Puritan colonizers eagerly desired to create a society strictly governed by biblical standards of justice and morality.[39] Earl Warren (1891–1974), a celebrated lawyer who served as the 30th Governor of California (1943–1953), and later as the 14th Chief Justice of the United States (1953–1969), expressed this undeniable truth in the following terms:

> I believe no one can read the history of our country without realizing that the good Book and the Spirit of the Savior have from the beginning been our guiding geniuses ... Whether we look to the first charter of Virginia ... or to the Charter of New England ... or to the Charter of Massachusetts Bay ... or to the Fundamental Orders of Connecticut ... the same objective is present: A Christian Land governed by Christian principles... I like to believe we are [still] living in the Spirit of the Christian religion. I like also to believe that as long as we do so, no great harm can come to our country. [40]

---

[38] Ibid., p 250.
[39] A. James Richley, *Religion in American Public Life* (Washington/DC: The Brookings Institution, 1985), p 55.
[40] Former Chief Justice Earl Warren, Address to the Annual Prayer Breakfast, International Conculd of Christian Leadership, 1954. Quoted from Gary DeMar, *Christian History: The Untold History* (Atlanta/GA: American Vision, 1995), p 1. '

15

The Revolutionary Period

During the second half of the eighteenth century, the colonists grew dissatisfied with English rule for a variety of reasons. Notably, England began to demand excessive taxes from them.[41] Furthermore, the English government began to impose their own courts so that the colonists began to gradually see the English government as generally behaving more like oppressive imperialists. By this time, not only had the colonies become vastly more sophisticated but a sense of being American had been more fully developed. Thus the imposition of English law and custom, imperfect in its application to the American situation, was perceived as unjust and stirred considerable discontent. This sentiment spread to all the colonies and eventually led to the outbreak of the American War of Independence in 1776.[42]

When analysing the prevailing ideologies during the American revolutionary period, it is evident that the colonists blended their political ideas with strong Christian motivations; indeed, Christianity was the underlying foundation of America's

---

[41]   Alain Levasseur & John S Baker (eds), *An Introduction to the Law of the United States* (New York : University Prless of America, 1992), p 3.
[42]   Ibid.

colonial law and culture in the eighteenth century. So it is not a surprise that Christian values turned out to be the leading inspiration that propelled the colonial leaders into declaring war against their British colonisers. By the time of the American Revolution, the people of the colonies generally believed that the British government was unlawfully attempting to suppress their 'inalienable' rights to life, liberty and property, and, thus, were violating God's 'Higher Law'.

The American Founders rejected English rule by relying primarily on the legal-political theories of John Locke, William Blackstone and the Baron of Montesquieu. These leaders essentially viewed the actions of the British government as contravening the Christian concept of natural law and, as such, God-given inalienable rights. Their Revolutionary War was perceived as a just form of civil disobedience since continued obedience to the British government was deemed an unlawful violation of the 'higher powers' and the 'common good'.[43] The constitutional principle of placing the English monarch under a Christian system of government fitted this context. For instance, regarding the 'duties' of Christian monarchs, William Tyndale (1494-1536) had already taught a few centuries earlier in England that they ought to 'give themselves to the wealth [welfare] of their realms after the ensample of Christ.' The Christian monarch, Tyndale concluded,

> shall remember ... that the people are God's, not theirs', and that 'the king is but a servant to execute the law of

---

[43] Kermit L. Hall, William Wiecek, and Paul Finkelman, *American Legal History: Cases and Materials* (2nd Ed) (New York/NY: Oxford University Press, 1996), p 58.

God, and not to rule after his own imagination.[44]

The support of the Christian church to the revolutionary cause was nothing short of remarkable. Throughout that period countless priests advised their congregations that they not only had a moral duty but, above all, a biblical mandate to resist political tyranny. For example, the Reverend Jonathan Mayhew, a minister of the Massachusetts Congregational Church, delivered a widely printed and celebrated sermon in 1750, which was distributed across all the colonies. The sermon exemplified the general sentiment among the colonists, declaring that

> [a]ll commands running counter to the declared will of the Supreme Legislator of Heaven and Earth are null and void, and therefore disobedience to them is a duty, not a crime … We have learned from the Holy Scriptures that the Son of God came down from heaven to make us free indeed, and … where the Spirit of the Lord is, there is liberty.[45]

This direct appeal to the Holy Scriptures to justify revolutionary action reflected Christianity's prevailing influence and perception of the law. Founded on St Paul's admonition in Romans 13:1 ('Let every soul be subject unto the higher power … the powers that be are ordained of God'), Reverend Mayhew's sermon applied biblical principles of government so as to conclude that '[c]ommon tyrants and public oppressors are not entitled to obedience from their subjects by virtue of

---

[44] William Tyndale, *The Obedience of a Christian Man* (London/UK: Penguin, 2000), p. 63. William Tyndale (1494-1536) became a leading figure in the Protestant Reformation in the years leading up to his execution. He is well known for his translation of the Bible into English. For such a 'crime' of translating the Bible into English, he was condemned to death. On October 6, 1536, Tyndale was strangled and his body burned at the stake. His last prayer was "Lord, open the King of England's eyes."

[45] Gragg, above n.18, p 31.

anything here laid down by the inspired apostle.'[46] Mayhew emphasised, in his own words:

> [T]hat the apostle's argument is so far from proving it to be the duty of people to obey and submit to such rulers as act in contradiction to the public good, and so to the design of their office, that it proves the direct contrary. For, please to observe, that if the end of all civil government be the good of society; if this be the thing that is aimed at in constituting civil rulers; and if the motive and argument for submission to government be taken from the apparent usefulness of civil authority, - it follows, that when no such good end can be answered by submission, there remains no argument or motive to enforce it; and if, instead of this good end's being brought about by submission, a contrary end is brought about, and the ruin and misery of society effected by it, here is a plain and positive reason against submission in all such cases, should they ever happen. And therefore, in such cases, a regard to the public welfare ought to make us withhold from our rulers that obedience and submission which it would otherwise be our duty to render to them...[47]

The colonisers' abuse of powers left the colonists feeling largely disenfranchised. The British government had imposed excessive and unjustifiable taxes, ultimately at the expense of the 'New World' colonies. This sentiment was expressed in James Otis's influential essay *The Rights of the British Colonies* (1764), wherein he addressed the British government's 'unjust laws', thus conveying most colonialists' dual-patriotism. They still regarded themselves primarily as British subjects. Although the Americans were gradually developing their own

---

[46] Hall, Wiecek, and Finkelman, above n.43, p 58.
[47] Ibid, p 59.

local identity, they claimed rights that were largely deemed 'revolutionary' and anti-British by their colonisers.[48] Still, according to Otis, loyalty to England, and further recognition of British sovereignty, did not warrant displacing the inalienable rights of the American colonists and, in fact, all humankind, 'which by God and nature are fixed.'[49]

In August 1781, when the *Continental Congress* (a convention of delegates called together from all the colonies to form a governing body during the American Revolution) received the good news of the British surrender at Yorktown, which effectively signalled the end of the 'War of Independence', its elected members assembled for a worship service in a church in Philadelphia. Almost immediately after this that very Congress enacted legislation which instructed all the people from the 'liberated colonies' to observe a nationwide day of 'Public Thanksgiving and Prayer' for their remarkable victory. The legislation declared:

> Whereas it hath pleased Almighty God, father of mercies, remarkably to assist and support the United States of America in their important struggle for liberty against the long continued efforts of a powerful nation; it is the duty of all rankers to observe and thankfully acknowledge the interpositions of his Providence in their behalf. Through the whole of this contest, form its first rise to this time, the influence of Divine Providence may be clearly perceived in many signal instances.[50]

But the final victory of the Continental Army (i.e., the American revolutionary forces) was achieved only in 1783

---

[48] Ibid, p 60.
[49] Ibid.
[50] Gragg, above n.18, p 2.

with the signing of the final peace treaty with Britain.[51] The importance afforded to the Christian religion is patently visible in the framing of the peace treaty, which started with the following affirmation: 'In the name of the Most Holy and Undivided Trinity. It having pleased the Divine Providence to dispose the hearts of ... Prince George the Third, by the grace of God, king of Great Britain, France, and Ireland, defender of faith ...'.[52] The invocations to the 'Holy and Undivided Trinity' and 'Divine Providence' further proved the primacy of Christianity. The treaty even goes as far as declaring that the end of the conflict, and the independence of the Americans, was ordained by 'the grace of God'.

---

[51] Geoffrey R. Stone, et al, *Constitutional Law* (Boston/MA: Little, Brown and Company, 1986), p 1.
[52] *Paris Peace Treaty* (1783).

16

Prevailing Philosophical Influences During the American Revolutionary Period

A few years ago political theorists from the University of Houston and Louisiana State Universities carried out comprehensive-research to identify the American Founders' most quoted sources. After a decade of research, and more than 15,000 writings from the founding era, 3,154 citations were counted. The Founders' often quoted three persons in particular: Baron Charles de Montesquieu, Sir William Blackstone, and John Locke. Lord Coke's Second Reports was also a major reference. However, and much to the surprise of these researchers, they discovered that the Founders' most quoted source was the Bible. Indeed, the Bible appears in no less than 34 per cent of all the quotes made by them. Another 60 per cent of the Founders' quotations are from authors who were actually quoting the Bible. Empirically, 94 per cent of all their quotations were based on the Bible either directly or indirectly.[53]

On the eve of the War of Independence no profession was more influential in colonial society than the clergy. Colonial

[53]   H Wayne House (ed.), *The Christian and American Law: Christianity's Impact on America's Founding Documents and Future Direction* (Kregel Publications, 1998), p 85.

America was a faith-centred society wherein people flocked to the churches to receive religious direction. While some pastors counselled loyalty to the British government (in particular those affiliated to the Church of England) many more denounced 'taxation without representation' as a visible sign of political tyranny and violation of God-given rights.[54] And it is quite remarkable that about half of all the signers of the Declaration of Independence were active members of the Church of England![55] As can be seen, the support for independence was certainly not limited to the Reformed or Calvinist denominations.

The politics of America's formative era were guided by the political inheritance from Britain, and the moral values that the Founders 'took from the King James Bible and the Book of Common Prayer.'[56] Congregationalists, Baptists and Lutherans also supported the Revolution. Even the small population of Roman Catholics primarily based in Maryland[57] generally supported the revolutionary efforts, believing that a fully independent America – even if overwhelmingly Protestant – 'offered greater religious freedom than Great Britain.'[58] The tiny Jewish community shared the same view. The Jewish merchant

---

[54] Gragg, above n.18, p 30.

[55] Ibid, p 69.

[56] Russell Kirk, *Rights and Duties: Reflections on our Conservative Revolution* (Dallas/TX: Spence Publishing Co., 1997), p 38.

[57] 'From the other end of European religious spectrum, Maryland was established in 1634 as a refuge for English Catholics. Its founders, George Calvert and his son Cecilius, had converted to Catholicism after service to James I, who with his son Charles I awarded them the colony in gratitude. Protestants always made up the bulk of Maryland's settlers, and after the Catholic James II was deposed, the colony in 1691 came under Anglican rule. Yet throughout the colonial period, Maryland offered an unusual sanctuary for Catholics in a British world marked by extreme prejudice against Rome'. – Noll, above n.12, p 394.

[58] Ibid, p 70.

and financier, Haym Salomon, donated a small fortune to the war effort. He lived in Philadelphia and was left 'practically penniless at the time of his death in 1785.'[59] Despite all these religious differences, Cragg explains:

> Colonial Americans – Protestant, Catholic, and Jewish – were united by their common identity and by the biblical perspective they shared. Already America was a 'melting pot' of people – still predominately English, but seasoned with Scots, Irish, Germans, Dutch, French, Africans, and others. Beneath this New World garden of cultures, however, America was unified by the bedrock foundation of the Judeo-Christian worldview.[60]

16.1. John Calvin (1509-1564)

John Calvin was a French theologian, pastor and reformer in Geneva during the Protestant Reformation. Since Christ himself stated that to love and honour God is the first and greatest commandment, he concluded that 'all authorities who betray their office to the detriment or defamation of God forfeit their office and are reduced to private persons. They are not long authorities but mere 'brigands' and 'criminals'. Also, according to Calvin: 'Dictatorship and unjust authorities are not governments ordained by God ...; those who practice blasphemous tyranny are no longer God's ministers.'[61] Against such an 'overbearing tyranny', Calvin concluded, Christians

---

[59] Ibid, p 74.
[60] Ibid.
[61] *Institutes* (1536) 6.56; Comm. Rom. 13:1-7; Commentary on Acts 5:29, 7:17. Quoted from John Witte Jr., 'Calvinist Contributions to Freedom in Early Modern Europe', *in* Timothy Samuel Shah and Allan D. Hertzke (eds.), *Christianity and Freedom – Volume I: Historical Perspectives* (Cambridge University Press, 2016), p 212.

must 'venture boldly to groan for freedom'.[62] As Calvin put it,

> Earthly princes lay aside their power when they rise up against God and are unworthy to be reckoned among the number of mankind. We ought rather utterly to defy them than obey them.[63]

Calvin believed that political legitimacy rests on laws and agreements, preferably written, which are necessary for protecting the 'freedom of the people', a term he frequently invoked. Written law, he argued, 'is nothing but an attestation of the [natural law], whereby God bring back to memory what has already been imprinted in our hearts'.[64] Thus he endorsed civil resistance against tyrannical rulers who attempt to violate the fundamental rights that undergird the founding agreement between the people and their political rulers, and which comprise an imprescriptible limit on governmental power. These fundamental rights are related to the second table of the Decalogue, stressing the need for legal protection of our God-given rights to life, liberty and property, as well as the right of free conscience.[65]

In *Commentary on the Acts of the Apostles* (1552-54) Calvin comments: 'It is in fact possible to claim that we are not violating the authority of the king' in any case where 'our religion compels us to resist tyrannical edicts.'[66] Presentation of this point is further elaborated in *A Short Treatise of Political Power* by the Calvinist priest John Ponet (1514-56). Appointed Archbishop

---

[62]   Ibid, p 213.
[63]   John Calvin, Commentary on Daniel, Lecture 30. Quoted from Robin Gill, *A Textbook of Christian Ethics* (London/UK: Bloomsbury, 2014), p 141.
[64]   Calvin's Commentary on the Psalms, ch.119, cited in Little, above n.36, p 225.
[65]   Ibid.
[66]   Quentin Skinner, *The Foundations of Modern Political Thought, Volume 2: The Age of Reformation* (Cambridge University Press, 1978), p 220.

of Winchester in 1551, this Anglican minister was forced to resign after the accession of Queen Mary only two years later. Ponet argued that political rulers are 'ordered to do good, not to do evil' since they are the ministers of God 'to punish the evil and to defend the good.'[67] He insisted that since these rulers are 'but executors of God's laws', no law enacted by them can be 'contrary to God's law and the laws of nature.' With citations from both the civil and canon law, a chapter in his book is titled 'whether it be lawful to depose an evil governor and kill a tyrant'. This chapter informs that, 'if a prince robs and spoils his subjects, it is theft, and as a theft ought to be punished.' 'If he kills and murders them [in such a manners as to be] contrary or without the [fundamental] laws of his country, it is murder, and as murderer he ought to be punished.'[68] As noted by the British political philosopher Quentin Skinner,

> [t]he theory of popular revolution developed by the radical Calvinists in the 1550s was destined to enter the mainstream of modern constitutionalist thought. If we glance forward more than a century to John Locke's *Two Treatises of Government* – the classic text of radical Calvinist politics – we find the same set of conclusions being defended, and to a remarkable extent by the same arguments.[69]

In the seventeenth century the language of 'natural rights' was understood by the Calvinists to apply equally to every human being. Any violation of these moral constraints could justify, in extraordinary circumstances, 'duly restrained counterforce against them'.[70] Calvinists taught that there are

---

[67]   Ibid, p 222.
[68]   Ibid, p 223.
[69]   Ibid, p 239.
[70]   Little, above n.36, p 185.

two covenants, one between God and the community (including the ruler and the people as parties), and another between the ruler and the people. Since such covenants are seen in terms of advancing the predictability, reasonableness, and security that is emphasised in the law of property and contract,[71] this ultimately led to the Puritan revolt against the 'tyranny' of Charles I, in the 1640s.[72]

It is not difficult to understand why American Calvinist groups were the more fervent supporters of independence from the United Kingdom, particularly the Presbyterians. Few people in the colonial period could match their revolutionary fervour. Some of them were the proud descendants of English Puritans who had fought a century earlier in the English Civil War against the English monarchy. Like their Puritan forebears, those Calvinists who led America's War of Independence 'frequently compared their own struggle with Great Britain to that of Israel's contest against Egypt.'[73] In broad terms their Calvinism emphasised the need to teach people the civil morality of common human duty, as well as the spiritual morality of biblical aspirations.[74] They believed that everyone is

---

[71] Harold J. Berman, 'Law and Belief in Three Revolutions' (1984) 18 (3) *Valparaiso University Law Review* 569, p 607.

[72] As noted by David Little, 'The Puritans claimed that the Stuart monarchy had become grossly arbitrary, and thus thoroughly illegitimate, in part because it had systematically violated the rights of its citizens. In the name of restoring those rights, appeals to which had become widespread in the seventeenth century, the government needed first to be restrained by forceful means as necessary and thereafter be drastically restructured'. – Little, above n.36, p 185.

[73] David G. Dalin, 'Jews, Judaism, and the American Founding', *in* Daniel L. Dreisbach and Mark David Hall (eds.), *Faith and the Founders of the American Republic* (New York/NY: Oxford University Press, 2014), p 64.

[74] John Witte, Jr, 'Introduction', John Witte, Jr and Frank S Alexander (eds), *Christianity and Law: An Introduction* (Cambridge/UK: Cambridge University Press, 2008), p 23.

a sinner falling short of God's glory, and to prevent the spread of immoral behaviour we all need the restraint of the law to drive us into repentance and, ultimately, full reconciliation with God. As John Witte, Jr, points out:

> The doctrine of sin ... influenced early modern Calvinists' insights into the nature of rights and their constitutional protection. It was their doctrine of sin that led Calvinists from the state to emphasize the need both for individual discipline and for structural safeguards on offices of authority.[75]

Under the influence of Calvinist philosophy the American Founders were taught since childhood about the pre-eminence of the 'higher law' at home and church. They were persuaded to believe that both the king and Parliament violated the rule of law if they ever attempted to subvert God-given 'natural rights' to life, liberty and property.[76] Such a doctrine, in turn, laid the foundations for constitutional theories of liberal democracy and basic human rights.[77] As also noted by Witte, Jr:

> The political office must be protected against the sinfulness of the political official. Political power, like ecclesiastical power, must be distributed among self-checking executive, legislative, and judicial branches. Officials must be elected to limited terms of office. Laws must be clearly codified, and discretion closely guarded. If officials abuse their office, they must be disobeyed. If they persist in their abuse, they must be removed even by revolutionary force and regicide. These Protestant teachings were among the driving ideological forces behind the revolts of the French Huguenots, Dutch Pietists, and Scottish Presbyterians

---

[75] Ibid., p 23.
[76] Gragg, above n.18, p 71.
[77] Witte, above n.74, p 24.

against their monarchical oppressors in the sixteenth and seventeenth centuries. They were critical weapons in the arsenal of the revolutionaries in England and America, and important sources of inspiration and instruction during the great age of democratic construction in later eighteenth- and nineteenth-century North America and Western Europe.[78]

16.2. Sir Edward Coke (1552-1634)

Another remarkable philosophical influence during the revolutionary period was Sir Edward Coke's *Institutes of the Laws of England*. First published in 1604, the second volume of Coke's *Institutes* is broadly recognised as the classical statement of English constitutional principles in the seventeenth century. The volume covers 39 statutes of significance that affected the rights and liberties of the English people. The most significant of these is undoubtedly Coke's famous commentary on Magna Carta. It soon became incredibly influential not just in England but also in North America, and, later still, in all the other countries of the British Empire. Due in great part to Coke's influential writings on Magna Carta, it was not only in England that the charter acquired a profound influence on constitutional development. In the New World, Magna Carta was adopted as the basis for the first charters that were taken across the Atlantic with the first English colonialists.

Lord Coke's writings on Magna Carta had been published in the colonies as early as 1687. It is primarily due to Coke's interpretation of the document that the Americans turned for inspiration when revolution swept through the continent. No

---

[78] Ibid, p 4.

tax without consent; no imprisonment without due process; such were the issues that lay beneath the 1776 Declaration of Independence as the colonies wrenched themselves free from British rule. As Dan Jones puts it, '[t]he colonists saw themselves as English freemen, whose rights were to be afforded precisely the same protection as those in the old country.'[79]

Curiously, Coke was deeply active in setting legal and commercial frameworks for the ventures in North America, playing an essential role in the draft of the first charter of Virginia Company, in 1606. This charter declared that the English settlers had the constitutional right to enjoy 'all liberties, franchises, and immunities ... as if they had been abiding and born within this our realm of England.'[80] The liberties of Englishmen were further guaranteed in the charters of Massachusetts (1629), Maryland (1632), Connecticut (1662), Rhode Island and Carolina (both 1663) and Georgia (1732).

Coke argued that Magna Carta 'was for the most part declaratory of the principal grounds of the fundamental laws of England, and for the residue it is additional to supply some defects of the common law'; again, that 'this statute of Magna Carta is but a confirmation or restitution of the Common Law'; and again, in Clause 29, that 'this chapter is but declaratory of the old law of England.'[81] This view served as the primary inspiration for the draft of the American Bill of Rights and all its colonial predecessors.[82] Influenced by Coke's interpretation,

---

[79] Dan Jones, *Magna Carta: The Making and Legacy of the Great Charter* (Head of Zeus, 2014), p 111.
[80] Nicholas Vincent, *Magna Carta: A Very Short Introduction* (Oxford/UK: Oxford University Press, 2014), p 93.
[81] Sir Edward Coke, *The First Part of the Institutes of the Laws of England* (1268).
[82] Paul O Carrese, *The Cloaking of Power: Montesquieu, Blackstone, and the Rise of Judicial Activism* (University of Chicago Press, 2003) p 185.

the American revolutionaries regarded Magna Carta as the fundamental statement of English liberties, and a symbol and reminder of constitutional principles binding on every governmental action.[83] According to law professor Joyce Lee Malcolm of George Mason University,[84]

> Americans ... remained wedded to Sir Edward Coke's assurance that a royal command or parliamentary statute that violated a right was void. No one need, or ought to obey it. This view was especially compelling for Americans, since they opposed those parliamentary statutes infringing on promised rights and resented having no representation in that body. The American mindset, therefore, remained fixed on early seventeenth-century ideas that fundamental liberties embedded in Magna Carta and in common law needed to be jealously guarded and the appropriate means to protect them. These means included individual challenges and civil disobedience; the refusal of officials to carry out acts repugnant to rights; judges ready to declare any violation of a right against law; and finally nullification by juries.[85]

The influence of biblical jurisprudence was at its height in England during the period when the American colonies were being most actively settled. The presence of Coke's doctrine in North America led the colonial legislatures to seek efforts to secure for their constituencies all the benefits of Magna Carta,

---

[83]   Edward S. Corwin, *The Higher Law Background of American Constitutional Law* [1928] (Indianapolis/IN: Liberty Fund, 2008), p 69.

[84]   Joyce Lee Malcolm is the Patrick Henry *Professor of Constitutional Law at George Mason University Law School*. She is a historian and constitutional scholar specializing in British and Colonial American History. She focuses on the development of individual rights and has written extensively on the subject.

[85]   Joyce Lee Malcolm, 'Magna Carta in America: Entrenched', *in* Nicholas Vincent (ed.), *Magna Carta: The Foundation of Freedom 1215-2015* (2nd ed., London: Third Millennium Publishing, 2015), p 130.

particularly of Clause 29 which guarantees due process of law and trial by jury. As the late constitutionalist Edward S. Corwin pointed out, thanks to Coke's interpretation of Magna Carta the Americans were able to approach the 'law of the land' provision of Clause 29 as an affirmation not only of legislative supremacy but also of individual rights and liberties.[86] Further, the constant evocation of Magna Carta during the American colonial period (as a basic provider for political autonomy and the basic rights of the individual) 'served to fix terminology for the future moulding of thought.'[87]

Since the English colonies in the 'New World' were far from the seat of justice at Westminster and the Inns of Courts, American lawyers had to rely on printed law books and additions to the various abridgements that summarized important cases. These texts of the common law in North America were primarily the

---

[86]   Corwin, above n.83, p 69. Edward S. Corwin (1878-1963) was the third Mc-Cormick Professor of Jurisprudence and first chairman of the Department of Politics at Princeton University. He was also the President of the prestigious American Political Science Association and considered the leading expositor of the intent and meaning of the U.S. Constitution. According to Corwin, Coke interpreted 'by the law of the land [per legen terrae]' to mean 'by the Common Law, Statute Law, or Custome of England'. Such interpretation was given on the basis of 'due process of law', a term which appears for the first time in Statute 37 of Edward III, in 1344, when the English Parliament compelled the king to consent to a statute law curbing his royal prerogative. The section is worth reproducing: 'No man of what estate or condition that he be, shall be put out of law or tenement, nor taken nor imprisoned, nor disinherited nor put to death without being brought in answer by due process of law.' The same expression, 'due process', would be enshrined in the Fifth Amendment to the U.S. Constitution, which declares that no-one 'shall be deprived of life, liberty, or property without a due process of law'. A similar provision is later found in the Fourteenth Amendment, which was enacted after the American Civil War, in 1868. This Amendment forbids any state-member of the American Federation to 'deprive any person of life, liberty or property without due process of law, nor deny to any person within its jurisdiction the equal protection of the laws'.

[87]   Corwin, above n.83, p 69.

works of Coke, which the *Commentaries* of William Blackstone supplemented.[88] According to Thomas Jefferson, Coke's *Institutes* was 'the universal law of book students, and a sounder Whig never wrote, nor of profounder learning in the orthodox doctrines of the British Constitution, or in what was called British liberties.'[89] Jefferson wrote this about *Institutes*: 'This work is executed with so much learning and judgement, that I do not recollect that a single position in it has ever been judicially denied. And ... it may still [1814] be considered as the fundamental code of English law.'[90]

An important document in American legal history was published on 12 September 1765: 'Summary of Disorders in the Massachusetts Province proceeding from an Apprehension that the Act of Parliament called the Stamp Act deprives the People of their Natural Rights'. Written by Lieutenant-Governor Hutchinson, it reveals his view that the Americans were taking 'advantage of a maxim they find in Lord Coke that an Act of Parliament against Magna Carta or the peculiar rights of Englishmen is *ipso facto* void.' Hutchinson then complains about a resolution of the Massachusetts's Legislative Assembly declaring the Stamp Act (a tax introduced by an Act of the British Parliament on 22 March 1765) 'against Magna Charta and the natural rights of Englishmen, and therefore according to Lord Coke null and void.'[91] Through Coke, the colony's

---

[88]   James R. Stoner, *Common Law and Liberal Theory: Coke, Hobbes, and the Origins of American Constitutionalism* (University Press of Kansas, 1992), p 13.
[89]   Andrew Lipscomb (ed.), *The Writings of Thomas Jefferson* (Washington/DC: Thomas Jefferson Memorial Association, 1903), p xii.
[90]   Samuel Thorne, *Sir Edward Coke, 1552-1592* (London/UK: Bernard Quaritch, 1957), p 3.
[91]   Quoted in Theodore F. T. Plucknett, 'Bonham's Case and Judicial Review', in Allen D. Boyer (ed.), *Law, Liberty and Parliament: The Selected Essays on the Writings of Sir Edward Coke* (Indianapolis/IN: Liberty Fund, 2004), p 179.

legislative assembly asserted that every person in America was entitled to the same rights as an Englishman; rights which are guaranteed in Magna Carta according to Coke's interpretation and the spirit of that historical document.

The colonial judiciary often cited Coke as a source of authority for interpreting the principles of the common law. Hence, in *Trevett v Weeden* (1768) the Superior Court of Rhode Island relied on Coke's authority to declare the unconstitutionality of an act of the local legislature imposing penalties on anyone who refused to take the state's paper money at its face value. The legislation empowered that court and the Court of Common Pleas to try offenders without trial by jury. Four judges, including the Chief Justice, held such an act invalid while only one judge doubted the court's jurisdiction. The almost unanimous decision held the law void, thus relying on the plaintiff's argument that 'that great oracle of the law, Lord Coke' taught that legislative acts that are 'repugnant and impossible' must be declared 'null and void', including statutory law requiring judges to proceed 'without jury ... according to the law of the land.'[92]

In *Robin et al. v Hardway* (1772) the Superior Court of Virginia was called to decide on the fate of several persons of Indian descent who attempted to vindicate their freedom regardless of a statute of 1682 (and others) that apparently reduced them to slavery. Although the court held that such a statute had been repealed in 1705, the court took the opportunity to 'throw considerable light upon the legal thought of the period.'[93] The argument given reveals the profound impact of Coke's

---

[92] Ibid, p 182.
[93] Ibid, p 181.

interpretation of the common law in colonial America. Both the court and the plaintiffs found it proper and convenient to directly rely on Coke's reasoning in *Bonham's Case* and *Calvin's Case* to ultimately question the validity of an Act of Parliament:

> All acts of legislature apparently contrary to right and justice are, in our laws, and must be in the nature of things, considered as void. The laws of nature are the laws of God, whose authority can be superseded by no power on earth. A legislature must not obstruct our obedience to Him from Whose punishments they cannot protect us. All human constitutions which contradict His laws, we are in conscience bound to disobey. Such have been the adjudications of our courts of justice ... 8 Co. 118a Bonham's Case. Hob. 87. 7 Co. 14 Calvin's Case.[94]

In October 1774, the delegates to the first Continental Congress of the thirteen discontented colonies justified their grievances on grounds that the people of those colonies were acting as Englishmen, and as their ancestors in like cases have usually done.[95] Because the leaders of that revolution relied on Coke's influence and authority, when John Adams asserted that the English Parliament had no authority over the colonies, and that each colony comprised a separate power with its own independent legislature, he quoted verbatim from Coke's *Institutes*. His fellow Bostonian James Otis, in arguing against writs of assistance, raised a case based on Coke's assertion in *Bonham's Case* that it is lawful for the courts to control certain acts of Parliament, even to the extent of voiding them.[96] Otis

---

[94] Ibid, p 179.
[95] Jones, above n.79, p 111.
[96] See Thomas G Barnes, 'Introduction to Coke's 'Commentary on Littleton" in A D Boyer (ed), *Law, Liberty, and Parliament: Selected Essays on the Writings of Sir Edward Coke* (Indianapolis/IN: Liberty Fund, 2004) p 25.

relied on such writings of Coke to conclude that British policy was unlawfully depriving the American people of their fundamental rights derived from Magna Carta.

Under the influence of Coke's writings, the fundamental principles of Magna Carta were embedded first into the laws of the American states, then into the U.S. Constitution, and then into the American Bill of Rights. Ratified in 1791, the Bill of Rights – the first ten amendments to the U.S. Constitution – echoes Magna Carta in several places. For example, the Fifth Amendment ('no person shall … be deprived of life, liberty, or property, without due process of law'), is a reformulation of Clause 39 of the 1215 version of Magna Carta, which states: 'No free man is to arrested, or imprisoned, or disseized, or outlawed, or exiled, or in any other way ruined, nor will we go or send against him, except by the legal judgment of his peers or by the law of the land.'

The Fifth Amendment to the United States' Constitution contains also the important declaration that no person must be 'deprived of life, liberty, or property … nor shall private property be taken for public use, without justice compensation.' Compare this with the second half with Clause 30 of Magna Carta: 'No sheriff or bailiff of ours, or anyone else may take any free man's horses or carts for transporting things, except with the free man's agreement.' And the same can be said about the Sixth Amendment: 'In all criminal prosecutions, the accused shall enjoy the right to a speedy and public trial, by an impartial jury'. Compare this with Clause 40 of Magna Carta: 'To no one will we sell, to no one will we deny or delay, right or justice'. The similarities are striking, so 'it is perhaps no surprise that since the earliest years of the United States' existence, its citizens have looked upon Magna Carta with an almost Cokean enthusiasm ...'[97]

16.3. Algernon Sidney (1622-1683)

The practical advocacy of the first colonial leaders in America – Governor Winthrop, Roger Williams, and William Penn – was inspired by the writings of the Puritan political philosopher Algernon Sidney.[98] His political ideas epitomise more than any other the spirit of American republicanism. Sidney was a member of the Long Parliament and a leading political theorist in the seventeenth century. He eventually was executed in 1683 for plotting to overthrow the government of Charles II. A passionate advocate for natural rights and freedoms, Sidney famously argued 'that which is not just is not law, and that which is not law ought not to be obeyed ... For if natural liberty and natural law come from God, only one kind of community will satisfy God's law: a consent-based republic protecting the equal liberty of all'.[99]

Sidney supported the concept of lawful revolution against political tyranny. His writings inspired the urgent principles of the American Revolution: that all men are created equal; that just government rests on the consent of the governed; that government is instituted to secure the rights of human nature; and that there is a natural right to revolution against despotism.[100] The revolutionaries of 1776 warmly admired Sidney's principles and fighting republican spirit. His death

---

[97] Jones, above n.79, p 112.
[98] Ahlstrom, above n.14, p 129.
[99] Tahomas G. West, 'Foreword', in Algernon Sidney, *Discourses Concerning Government* (Indianapolis/IN: Liberty Fund, 1996), p xxiii.
[100] Ibid., p xxvi.

as a martyr to liberty provided the American Founders with a model in their own risky enterprise against the force of the British arms.[101] As noted by Thomas G. West, 'among those who cited Sidney prominently in their writings, besides [Thomas] Jefferson and [John] Adams, were Jonathan Mayhew, the spirited patriot preacher of Massachusetts, and Arthur Leer, a leading revolutionary politician of Virginia.'[102]

16.4. John Locke (1632-1704)

The work of the English philosopher John Locke played an enormously important role in the development of American constitutionalism. Locke is known as the 'Founder of Liberalism' due to his immense contributions to political philosophy, which provided moral-political justification for the Glorious Revolution in England. In the constitutional struggle of parliamentary forces against the Stuart monarchs in 17th-century England, the receptive attitude towards Biblical Christianity allowed philosophers like Locke to elaborate a theory in which the primary justification for civil government rests on the preservation of unalienable rights to life, liberty and property. Locke's main concern in his political writings was the elaboration of a legal-political philosophy to underpin the Glorious Revolution of 1688.

Of course, later in history his political philosophy is also reflected in the United States' Declaration of Independence, especially its appeal to God-given rights and the lawful right to resist tyranny. Although many commentators have expressed admiration for Locke's political philosophy as a major source

---

[101] Ibid.
[102] Ibid.

of classical liberal theory, it is important to observe that he 'explicitly based his entire thesis on Christian doctrines concerning moral equality.'[103] During his successful life as a philosopher and political theorist Locke supported a view of human equality (and dignity) that was deeply grounded in Christian philosophy.[104] The veracity of biblical teachings was a 'working premise' in Locke's political writings. The influence of such teachings is observable in his commentaries on property, family, slavery, government, and toleration.[105] According to Thomas G. West, he was 'a major theologian whose interpretation of Christianity was tremendously influential in Britain and America'.[106] Locke even wrote an apologetic work on the 'reasonableness' of Christianity. In respect to Locke's approach to the Christian religion, Victor Nuovo comments:

> Locke's Christianity was strongly messianic, which is to say, he believed that Christian doctrine must be understood as Scripture presents it, embedded in a sacred history that runs from the creation of Adam to the Last Judgement. In this connection, Locke adhered to the doctrine of divine dispensations. The proper place in this history to treat the themes of the *Two Treatises* is prior to the Mosaic theocracy and the founding of the messianic kingdom. The nature and function of the civil state are properly considered, then, only under the general providence of God which prevailed under the Adamic and Noachic dispensations.

---

[103] Rodney Stark, *Victory of Reason: How Christianity Led to Freedom, Capitalism and Western Success* (New York/NY: Random House, 2005), p 76.

[104] Jeremy Waldron, *God, Locke and Equality: Christian Foundations of John Locke's Political Thought* (Cambridge University Press, 2002), p 27-28.

[105] Ibid., p 151.

[106] Thomas G. West, 'The Transformation of Protestant Theology as a Condition of the American Revolution', in Thomas S. Engeman and Michael P. Zuckert (eds.), *Protestantism and the American Founding*, (University of Notre Dame Press, 2004), p 88.

> The counterpart of the *Two Treatises* is *The Reasonableness of Christianity*, whose central theme is the founding of the transcendent Kingdom of God. The difference between the two realms and their respective authorities is a central theme of the *Epistola de tolerantia*.[107]

Locke approached the area of theology as a 'science' that stood 'incomparably above all the rest'. As Alex Chafuen explains, 'it is hard to read any work by Locke that does not bring up God or the Bible'.[108] He even spent the last days of his life exclusively trying to better understand the Bible and all the benefits of Christianity. 'The honour and veneration of the Creator, and the happiness of mankind. This is that noble study which is every man's duty, and every one that can be called a rational creature is capable of', Locke wrote in 1697.[109] According to him, '[t]his is that science which would truly enlarge men's minds, were it studied, or permitted to be studied everywhere with that freedom, love of truth, and charity which it teaches, and were not made, contrary to its nature, the occasion of strife, faction, malignity, and narrow impositions.'[110]

Locke believed that no conflict must exist between reason and the Christian faith. He made a special effort to investigate not only the things that are more readily discoverable by reason, but also the things to be found through God's revelation. Locke stressed that 'every man has an immortal soul', and that reason

---

[107] Victor Nuovo, 'Review of Jeremy Waldron's God, Locke and Equality' (2003) 5 *Notre Dame Philosophical Reviews*, at http://ndpr.nd.edu/news/23410-god-locke-and-equality-christian-foundations-of-locke-s-political-thought/

[108] Chafuen, Alejandro A (Alex), 'John Locke: A Religious Champion of Freedom', *American Conservative Union*, 30 July 2010,

[109] John Locke, *The Conduct of the Understanding* [1697] (London/UK: M. Jones, 1802), p 73

[110] Ibid.

and common equity actually work together and in perfect harmony so as to provide the measure in which 'God has set for the actions of men for their mutual security'.[111] And the weakness of relying on reason alone (without the assistance of revelation) was also explained by him. [112]

When most Americans now seem so proud about living in a 'multicultural society', and secularist education is deemed the best for children, it is interesting to note that Locke supported a form of liberal education that teaches children to know the Bible and to trust in God. The reason as to why he considered important for children to know the Bible (before they enter in natural philosophy) is because, according to Locke, 'by reading of it constantly, there would be instilled into the minds of children a notion and belief of spirits, they having to do so much to do in all the transactions of that history, which will be a good preparation to the study of bodies. For without the notion and allowance of spirit, our philosophy will be lame and defective in one main part of it, when it leaves out the contemplation of the most excellent and powerful part of the creation'.[113] For Locke,

---

[111] John Locke, *The Reasonableness of Christianity* [1695] (Washington/DC: Gateway Editions, 1965) p. 21.

[112] John Milton, who is Emeritus Professor of the History of Philophy at King's College London, describes Locke's theological studies as follows: "Locke's theological reading during the early 1660s can be loosely divided into three categories: biblical scholarship, patristics, and Anglican theology. The first of these was an area in which Locke continued to work for the remainder of his life — the *Paraphrase* was the culmination of a lifetime's study, not a late intellectual deviation. The other two areas were of course connected — the study of the Church Fathers was always an Anglican rather than a Puritan activity. Locke seems, for whatever reason, to have been interested primarily in the earlier Fathers — Justin Martyr, Tertullian, Irenaeus, Clement of Alexandria, and Origen". – J.R. Milton, 'Locke at Oxford', *in* G. A. J. Rogers (ed.), *Locke's Philosophy: Content and Context* (Oxford University Press, 1994), p 42

[113] John Locke, *A Letter Concerning Toleration* [1685] (New York/NY: Walter J. Black, 1947), p 369

'it is evident that by mere matter and motion none of the great phenomena of nature can be resolved'. [114] He provides some examples to demonstrate his point, ultimately recommending:

> To prepare a good foundation for virtue in a child there ought very early to be imprinted on his mind a true notion of God, as of the independent Supreme Being, Author, and Maker of all things, from whom we receive all our good, who loves us, and gives us all things; and, consequent to it, a love and reverence of this Supreme Being. ... And I am apt to think, the keeping children constantly morning and evening to acts of devotion to God, as to their Maker, Preserver, and Benefactor, in some plain and short form of prayer, suitable to their age and capacity, will be of much more use to them in religion, knowledge, and virtue, than to distract their thoughts with curious inquiries into his inscrutable essence and being.[115]

Although an Anglican in faith, Locke was clearly influenced by Calvinism. Calvinist theology communicates the duty of lower magistrates to resist undue arbitrariness. According to Harold Berman, 'these and the other Calvinist teachings were invoked to support limitations placed on the English monarch in the Long Parliament in 1640 and during the Civil War that followed, the subjection of the monarchy to Parliament in the period after its restoration in 1660, and, finally, in 1688, the forced abdication of the monarch and his replacement by a new dynasty subject to the severe restrictions placed on it by the Bill of Rights of 1689'.[116] Locke derived from Calvinism his own theories about the natural law, the social compact, and

---

[114] Ibid.
[115] Ibid.
[116] Berman, above n.71, p 604.

government by consent of the governed.[117] As Berman also commented,

> Locke's theories of social contract and of government by consent of the governed, expounded in his Two Treatises of Government, published in 1689-90 as a justification of the Parliamentary system as established by the Glorious Revolution, were based essentially on liberal Calvinist doctrine. Underlying Locke's theory was the Calvinist emphasis on man's inherent selfishness. It was this that required the reciprocal limitation on power – on the power of subjects as well as on the power of rulers – that are implicit in the concept of a contract. [118]

During the colonisation period, Locke's political philosophy influenced 'state constitutions and most notably the Declaration of Independence, which was overtly theistic.'[119] Locke was understood as offering 'a political thought fully compatible with orthodox Christian belief'.[120] In his *Second Treatise* Locke argues that our most fundamental rights are independent of, and antecedent to, the emergence of civil government. To Locke, the state 'hath no other end but the preservation of these rights, and therefore can never have a right to destroy, enslave, or designedly to impoverish the subjects.' If a government exceeds the limits of its power, the people can dismiss the government for a breach of trust. t elaborates on a 'state of nature' predating the creation of the state in which people were ruled not by

---

[117] Harold J. Berman, 'Religious Foundations of Law in the West: An Historical Perspective' (1983)1 *Journal of Law and Religion* 3, p 29.

[118] Berman, above n.71, p 605.

[119] Michael V Hernandez, 'Theism, Realism, and Rawls' (2010) 40 *Seton Hall Law Review* 905, p 911.

[120] Matthew J. Franck, 'Christian and Freedom in the American Founding', in Timothy Samuel Shah and Allen D. Hertzke, *Christianity and Freedom – Volume I: Historical Perspectives* (Cambridge University Press, 2016), p 270.

positive laws but only by a natural law that everybody is able to recognise and uphold.[121] This 'law of nature', Locke explains,

> stands as an eternal rule to all men, legislators as well as others. The rules that they make for other men's actions must, as well as their own and other men's actions, be conformable to the law of nature, ie to the will of God of which that is a declaration. And the fundamental law of nature being the preservation of mankind, no sanction can be good or valid against it.[122]

Locke regarded the state of nature as a fictitious assumption, expedient as it was for answering the question of how the power of the state can be justified. Natural-law thinkers like him were not dealing with the historical antecedents of civil government; rather, they were focused on the idea of the state as an entity distinct from society, a legal-institutional association based on a contract (or written constitution) which provides for separation of powers as well as the basic rights and duties between the people and their rulers. Locke's answer begins by inferring a social condition which is prior to the advent of the first civil government. In such a 'state of nature', people have the right to enforce the law of nature and to punish wrongdoers for violating such a law. This right to punish wrongdoers according to natural law, however, conflicts with the principle that nobody is a good judge in his or her own cause. That so being, the enjoyment of one's natural rights in a state of nature

---

[121] We should not too readily dismiss Locke's theory of 'state of nature' as completely unhistorical and crudely individualistic. Natural law thinkers like him were not dealing with the historical antecedents of the state. Rather, a case can be made for the view that the state, as distinct from society, is a legal association that fundamentally rests on the assumption of a social contract (or written constitution) prescribing the basic rights and obligations of both the citizens and the state.

[122] John Locke, *Second Treatise of Government* (c 1681), Ch 11, sec 135.

is actually insecure.[123]

The Lockean model of 'state of nature' is not pre-social. People living under a state of nature are still settled in a social context and enjoy equal rights to property and recognise claims against one another. Although they are aware of their own rights, a certain bias of interest and lack of attention often causes them to apply the natural law more rigorously in the case of others than of themselves. Since the state of nature inevitably lacks an impartial agency to resolve legal disputes, crimes often go unpunished and such disputes tend toward a 'state of war' between the conflicting parties. Such problems ultimately justify the creation of a civil government in whom trust must be reposed. This is how a social contract is established. Such a contract must be created and, on such basis, a legitimate government can be constitution: to establish a civil authority endowed by the terms of the contract with the lawful authority to enforce the law that safeguards our natural rights to life, liberty and property.

On the basis of this fundamental premise, according to Locke, the state puts itself into a 'state of war' against society every time it attempts to undermine our basic rights and freedoms. Being God-given and inalienable, even if one seeks to bargain these rights away, one simply cannot succeed because natural rights are not the sort of things that can actually be bargained. Such rights to life, liberty and property *set limits* on civil authority, thus providing a lawful justification for civil resistance against political tyranny should they be violated. To the extent that the state does not recognise and protect these rights, it actually ceases to be a legitimate authority and the people can lawfully

---

[123] Ibid., sec 123

dismiss it for the breach of trust. As Locke himself put it:

> Whenever the legislators endeavour to take away and destroy the property of the people [that is, their rights to life, liberty and property], or to reduce them to slavery under arbitrary power, they put themselves into a state of war with the people, who are thereupon absolved from any further obedience, and are left to the common refuge which God hath provided for all men against force and violence.[124]

We should not be too readily in dismissing Locke's idea of 'state of nature' as completely un-historical. The 'Mayflower Compact' drafted by the English Puritans actually established a Lockean social contract. Prior to going ashore at Plymouth, on 21 November 1620, those on board of the Mayflower assembled in the cabin of their ship to elaborate a social compact designed to provide for a new society based on 'just and equal laws'. This contract would serve to secure unity and provide for the constitution of a Christian commonwealth in 'New England'. The document explicitly declared: 'In the name of God, Amen. We whose names are underwritten … by the grace of God … having undertaken, for the glory of God, and advancement of the Christian faith …'.[125]

Although insisting that there is 'only one way to heaven', Locke also stressed that everyone is responsible for finding 'the narrow way and the strait gate that leads to heaven.'[126] Because Locke thought that 'man cannot be forced to be saved',[127] he concluded that 'religious truth' (and, indeed, any other truth) cannot be imposed by the state: 'it must be left to individual

---

[124] Ibid, ch 19, sec 222.
[125] Ibid.
[126] Ibid, p 19.
[127] Ibid, p 32.

conscience and individual discernment.'[128] To Locke, freedom of speech and freedom of conscience are the very essence of the classical Christian defence of religious toleration. Curiously, such an understanding of religious tolerance is not grounded on any doubt about the 'truth', or sympathy to religious beliefs that Locke thought they should be tolerated. Instead, Locke was adamant that most of the opinions he proposed to tolerate were, in actual fact, 'false and absurd'.[129]

It is undisputable that Locke's defence of religious freedom ultimately inspired the drafters of the very first amendment to the U.S. Constitution to establish freedom of religion and the principle of church-state separation.[130] Ultimately, Locke believed that the Bible is a confirmation of natural law principles. 'To give a man a full knowledge of true morality, I would send him to no other book than the New Testament', he said.[131] Such an advocacy of religious freedom and other fundamental rights worked as a great source of inspiration for the American Founding Fathers. As we are going to see later in this volume, their Declaration of Independence was deeply marked by the influence of Locke's political teachings.

16.5. John of Salisbury (1120-1280)

John Locke's contributions to political philosophy are reflected, among other things, in the United States' Declaration

---

[128] Jeremy Waldron, *Liberal Rights: Collected Papers 1981-1991* (Cambridge/UK: Cambridge, 1993), p 98.
[129] John Locke, *A Letter Concerning Toleration* (London: John Horton and Susan Mendus, 1991), p 41.
[130] Ibid, p 42-3.
[131] John Locke, *Essay Concerning Human Understanding* [1689] (New York/NY: Samuel Marks, 1825), p 256.

of Independence. And yet, it is curious to note that Locke's defence of religious freedom finds their early philosophical roots in John of Salisbury's distinction between 'a tyrant who oppresses the people by rulership based upon force' and 'a prince who rules in accordance with the laws'.[132] Born around 1120 Salisbury served as the Bishop of Chartres, in 1170, after serving first as Secretary to two celebrated Archbishops of Canterbury, first Theobald and then Thomas Becket. It was during this period that Salisbury composed his greatest treatise, the *Policraticus*, published in 1159. He was one of the leading medieval theologians to argue not only for freedom of religion but also absolute freedom of political speech. Writing between 1157 and 1159, his defence of free speech was entirely based on the Christian observation that virtue 'does not arise with perfection without liberty'.[133] Thus Salisbury mounted a powerful Christian argument for freedom of expression: '[I]t is the part of the good and wise man to give a free reign to the liberty of others, and to accept with patience the words of free speaking, whatever they might be'.[134]

The central part of Salisbury's impressive work (Books 4, 5, and 6) appeals directly to biblical principles and philosophy that exhort the kings to be respectful of their lawful duties. The difference between a lawful king and an evil tyrant, Salisbury reasoned, is that the former 'is obedient to law, and rules his people by a will that places itself at their service.'[135]

---

[132] Quoted from: Corwin, above n.83, p 18.
[133] Chris Berg, *In Defence of Freedom of Speech: From Ancient Greece to Andrew Bolt* (Melbourne/Vic: IPA/Mannkal, 2012).
[134] John of Salisbury, *Policraticus* (ed. by Cary J. Nederman, *Worlds of Difference: European Discourses of Toleration c.1100*, Penn State University Press, 2000), VII, p 25.
[135] Ibid., IV.i, p 28.

Since lawful rulers are 'concerned with the burdens of the entire community', they must observe the moral duty to 'love justice, cherish equity, procure the utility of the republic, and in all matters prefer the advantage of others to [their] private will.' Although like all medieval thinkers Salisbury had a high opinion of royal authority, he thought that 'it is just for public tyrants to be killed and the people to be liberated for obedience to God.' Just as the lawful king 'is to be loved, venerated and respected' – because he is God's delegated authority that must reflect God's image of loving mercy and goodness – so is the tyrant the image of evil and depravity who is for the most part even to be killed'.[136]

16.6. Baron de Montesquieu (1689-1755)

One of the results of the American Revolution was the establishment of a republican government in which ultimate political sovereignty is placed in the hands of the people. This greatly diverges from the English tradition whereby the Parliament (and sometimes the Crown) has been recognised as the ultimate source of sovereignty. Further, the American structure of government is based on a more rigid separation of government powers between the legislative, executive and judicial branches of government, an arrangement that remains fundamental to the American constitutional order even to this day.

The separation of government branches, which the drafters of the United States Constitution designed, is commonly traced to the work of the French philosopher and political

---

[136] Ibid.

theorist, Charles-Louis de Secondat, Baron de La Brède et de Montesquieu.[137] First published in 1748, Montesquieu's most celebrated book, *The Spirit of the Laws*, soon received widespread public acclamation. Its first English translation in 1750 soon became very popular in America, particularly during the ratification debates for the U.S. Constitution. Those who supported the ratification, and those who argued against it, relied quite heavily on Montesquieu to justify their positions.

During the founding of the American Republic 'Montesquieu was an oracle'. James Madison, Thomas Jefferson, John Adams, and others consciously tried to apply his principles in creating a new political system. He was quoted by them more than any modern author (only the Bible trumped him).[138] As noted by Jeremy Kirk, '[a]t the Constitutional Convention, no man was quoted more frequently than Montesquieu ... It was from Montesquieu ... that the Framers obtained a theory of checks and balances and of the division of powers.'[139] Those Framers deliberately based their entire political system heavily on Montesquieu's idea of separation of powers, with clear distinctions between the legislative, executive and the judicial branches of government; a concept which endures as fundamental to American constitutionalism.[140]

Montesquieu was convinced that political and civil institutions are not abstractly ordained or agreed at any one moment; instead, 'laws grow slowly out of people's experiences with one another,

---

[137] See Corwin, above n.83, p 54.
[138] Fareed Zakaria, *The Future of Freedom: Illiberal Democracy at Home and Abroad* (New York/NY: WW Norton & Co, 2003), p 45.
[139] Kirk, above n.56, p 105.
[140] This is based on Montesquieu's classic work *The Spirit of the Laws*.

out of social customs and habits.'[141] According to Montesquieu, '[w]hen a people have pure and regular manners, their laws become simple and natural.' And yet, there are other significant passages in 'The Spirit of Laws' assuring the influence of the Christian religion on the author's legal-political philosophy. For example, Book XXIV, Chapter 3, states the following: 'The Christian religion is a stranger to mere despotic power, because the mildness so frequently recommended in the Gospel is incompatible with despotic rage with which a prince punishes his subjects, and exercises himself in cruelty.'[142] By comparison, he describes Islam in a rather uncomplimentary light:

> From the characters of the Christian and Mahometan religions, we ought, without any further examination, to embrace the one, and reject the other: for it is much easier to prove that religion ought to humanize the manners of men, than that any particular religion is true. It is a misfortune to human nature, when religion is given by a conqueror. The Mahometan religion, which speaks only by the sword, acts still upon men which that destructive spirit with which it was founded.[143]

In that same chapter where Montesquieu compares the Christian religion with the Islamic faith, one finds the statement that '[w]hile the Mahometan princes incessantly give or receive death, Christianity renders their princes less timid and consequently less cruel. The Christian princes consequently have more humanity: they are more disposed to be directed by laws, and more capable of perceiving that they cannot do whatever they please.'[144] Montesquieu's admiration and

---

[141] Kirk, above n.56, p 105.
[142] Montesquieu; *The Spirit of Laws*. Book XXIV, Chapter 3.
[143] Ibid, Chapter 4.
[144] Ibid, Chapter 3.

appreciation for the legacy of Christianity as a force for good is also evident in numerous other passages of his 'The Spirit of the Laws', such as:

> How admirable the religion, which, while it seems only to have in view the felicity of the other life, constitutes the happiness of this! ... We owe to Christianity, in government a certain political law, and in war a certain law of nations, benefits which human nature can never sufficiently acknowledge.[145]

In 'The Spirit of the Laws' Montesquieu approaches 'natural law' as a rule of reason encompassing God's superior law. This law is deemed 'natural' because it instructs everyone to distinguish right from wrong, to form their own consciences and to guide their actions according to the right path. Because the natural law goes according to nature and it is the final elaboration of a benevolent God, it does not constitute a restriction on individuals and societies, but it is a pre-requisite for their natural and healthiest functioning. This law must be superior and antecedent to all existing laws. And yet, Montesquieu recognises that some laws vary from time to time, in accordance to economic, political, geographical, and socio-cultural contexts. The legislator must therefore take into account the local habits and customs of the people before proceeding with the creation of new legislation. This assumption that positive laws ought to reflect the particularities of social life and of those who live by them earned Montesquieu the well-deserved title of "Father of Legal Sociology".

Despite the existence and superiority of natural laws, humans according to Montesquieu may disobey such laws as

---

[145] Ibid.

much as they can disobey any other law, including the laws which they themselves have created. As Montesquieu reminds us, 'constant experience shows us that every man invested with power is apt to abuse it, and to carry his authority as far as it will go.' To prevent this, he concludes, 'it is necessary from the very nature of things that power should be a check to power.'[146] Remarkably, such a notion of separation of powers is based on the biblical premise that humans are inherently sinful; that they inevitably contravene God's law. Montesquieu believed that separation of powers is essential to counteract the concentration of power since he regarded humanity as inherently corrupt and self-centred, which is clearly observed in this famous passage of *The Spirit of Laws*:

> Man, as a physical being, is like other bodies governed by invariable laws. As an intelligent being, he incessantly transgresses the laws established by God, and changes those of his own instituting. He is left to his private direction, though a limited being, and subject, like all finite intelligences, to ignorance and error.[147]

So it was logical for Montesquieu to conclude that society can only be protected from tyranny if the power of the state does not repose in the same political authority. With the power of the state effectively divided, if one branch becomes too evil or corrupt, then the others must remain righteous and be able to check the wayward influence.[148] This doctrine of separation of powers is rooted in the biblical concept found in Jeremiah, Chapter 19, where it is stated that human rulers tend to naturally

[146] Ibid, Book XI, Ch V.
[147] Ibid, Book I, Ch I.
[148] David Barton, *Original Intent: The Courts, the Constitution & Religion* (Aledo/TX: Wallbuilders, 2005), p. 215.

become corrupt if their powers are left unchecked. Relying on this belief, particularly in the idea of original sin, Montesquieu concluded that it is 'necessary from the disposition of things that power should be check of power.' According to Nick Spencer, the basic reason why Montesquieu elaborated his theory of checks-and-balances

> lies in that fundamental Christian conviction of inherent human fallibility. Perfect freedom and perfect order are unrealisable because our very nature makes them unrealisable. Put another way, because humans are sinful, we are apt to abuse our freedom in a way that harms others. Although we should use our freedom for the common good, we tend not to, preferring instead, even if unconsciously, to deploy it for our own ends, even when those ends damage others. We need political order to keep us in check.
>
> But what applies to political freedom applies also to political order. We are as liable to abuse political authority as we are freedom with even more deleterious effects. Political order, structure and authority are necessary but they too demand limitation. Thus a ruler's reign is always under law, his authority is under judgement and his power is limited, in particular by the need to respect and honour the relationship between the individual (or the Church) and God himself. It is this freedom that, historically, formed the basis of wider, political freedoms. Thus, just as political order necessarily constrains our freedom, religious and political freedom must undermine our order.[149]

The American Founders agreed with the premise and assumed that applying Montesquieu's doctrine of separation of

---

[149] Nick Spencer, *Freedom & Order: History, Politics & the English Bible* (London: Hodder & Stoughton, 2011), p. 11.

powers was vital to counteract the inherent problems associated with our sinful ambitions for power and glory. They believed in the inherently corruptibility of human nature and societies. As George Washington once explained, '[a] just estimate of that love of power and proneness to abuse it which predominates it the human heart, is sufficient to satisfy us for the truth of this position.' Thus he concluded: 'the importance of reciprocal checks in the exercise of political power by dividing and distributing it into different depositories ... has been evinced.'[150] The same idea is found in Alexander Hamilton's Federalist Paper No.15: 'Why has government been instituted at all? Because the passions of men will not conform to the dictates of reason and justice without constraint ... [T]he infamy of a bad action is to be divided among a number [rather] than ... to fall singly upon one.'[151] Ultimately, as Mark David Hall pointed out,

> America's founders believed that because humans are sinful it is dangerous to concentrate political power. The Constitution thus carefully separates powers and creates a variety of mechanisms whereby each institution can check the others. Critically, the power of the national government itself was limited by Article I, section 8. Indeed, the very notion of federalism ... was itself modelled after Reformed approaches to church governance (especially Presbyterianism) and New England civic arrangements which ... were themselves heavily influenced by Calvinist political ideas. It is noteworthy that the authors of the Connecticut compromise, Roger Sherman and Oliver Ellsworth, were both serious Reformed Christians who were leaders in their Congregational Churches.

---

[150] George Washington, *Address of George Washington, President of the United States* (Baltimore: Christopher Jackson, 1796), p.22.
[151] Alexander Hamilton, *The Federalist Papers*, n.15.

Enlightenment thinkers, on the other hand, gene embraced unicameralism and the centralization of pc in a national government.[152]

16.7. Sir William Blackstone (1723-1780)

Sir William Blackstone's magisterial *Commentaries on the Laws of England* was an instant best-seller in America. As Michael Schutt noted, '[t]he Founders knew the *Commentaries*, and, with the Bible and theological writings of the Reformers, it had a formidable influence on the shape of early American law.'[153] Indeed, the 1765 publication of Blackstone's *Commentaries* coincided with increasing fear among the American colonialists that the British government were trampling their basic rights. He would become one of the founding generation is most frequently cited authors.

Despite its focus on those few who were 'free men' in 1215, Blackstone contended that *Magna Carta* 'protected every individual of the nation in the free enjoyment of his life, his liberty, and his property, unless declared to be forfeited by the judgements of his peers or the law of the land', a blessing 'which alone would have merited the title that it bears of the great charter.' 'Every wanton and causeless restraint of the will of the subject, wether practiced by a monarch, a nobility, or a popular assembly, is a degree of tyranny', Blackstone stated.[154] Like Coke, he insisted that the common law did not

---

[152] Mark David Hall, 'Vindiciae, Contra Tyrannos', *in* Daniel L. Dreisbach and Mark David Hall (eds.), *Faith and the Founders of the American Republic* (New York/NY: Oxford University Press, 2014), p 53.
[153] Michael P. Schutt, *Redeeming Law: Christian Calling and the Legal Profession* (Downers Grove, Il: IVP Academic, 2007), pp 26-7.
[154] Quoted from Malcolm, above n.67, p 128.

create, but merely preserved, our natural rights to life, liberty and property. 'In Blackstone's account of English law there is something of Locke, and something of Montesquieu, but chiefly the inheritance of common law and equity.'[155] According to his main biographer, 'Blackstone's clearly-stated emphasis on the authority of law of natural and the absolute rights of individuals was of particular importance in formulating and defending the case for armed resistance to King George and his parliament.'[156]

Blackstone's *Commentaries* soon became the most revered and influential legal text in America during the eighteenth and nineteenth centuries. Blackstone commences his seminal work with an affirmation of the natural law. The American Founders relied very heavily on such an exposition of the natural law when adapting the English common law example to the American context in the eighteenth century. American political leaders and lawyers at the time of Constitutional Convention, in 1787, were avowed disciples of Blackstone. As Kirk pointed out, 'the Framers, with a few conceivable exceptions, believed in the reality of the natural law and had no intention of contravening natural law by the instrument they drew up at Philadelphia; nor did anyone suggest during the debates over ratification that the Constitution might in any way conflict with the old truths of the natural law.'[157]

The constant evocation of natural law doctrines characterised the early days of American Federation. The famous Virginian jurist who edited the famous 1803 American edition of Blackstone's *Commentaries*, St George Tucker, wrote

---

[155] Kirk, above n.56, p 107.
[156] Wilfred Prest, *William Blackstone: Law and Letters in the Eighteenth Century* (Oxford University Press, 2008), p 292.
[157] Kirk, above n.56, p 130.

in regard to natural law that 'no man nor set of men can have any natural, or inherent right, to rule over the rest.'[158] In the nineteenth century, the whole fight against slavery in America relied almost entirely on the concept of natural rights as exposed in Blackstone's legal philosophy. The free blacks who agitated for the emancipation of their people often invoked the narrative of liberation in the Book of Exodus whereby Moses led the captive Israelites to freedom. Influenced by that biblical narrative, but even more so by Blackstone's Christian teachings concerning the natural law (and natural rights), Abraham Lincoln, that great American President who abolished slavery in 1863, believed that our basic rights are God-given, not concessions of the state.[159]

Within this context, natural law was mirrored in the American judiciary as many judges relied on Blackstone's definition when adjudicating legal matters.[160] Blackstone's Christian view of the natural law was openly acknowledged and advocated by the two leading legal scholars of the formative years of American Law: Chancellor James Kent and Joseph Story, who was the first Dane Professor of Law at Harvard University and later Associate Justice of the United States Supreme Court. Justice Story, for instance, directly linked natural law to the fundamental rights of the individual, which 'are given by God, and cannot be encroached upon by human authority, without a criminal disobedience of the precepts of natural, as well as revealed religion.'[161] As Kirk noted, '[t]he two great American

[158] Ibid, pp 81–2.
[159] Ibid, p 81.
[160] Ibid.
[161] Joseph Story, *Commentaries on the Constitution of the United States* (Boston/MA: Little, Brown and Company, 1833) p 1399.

commentators point out that Christian moral postulates are intrinsically woven into the fabric of the common law, and cannot be dispensed with, there being no substitute for them in ethical matters.'[162]

Law professor Albert W Alschuler reminds us that 'Blackstone taught American Revolutionaries their rights, helped inspire the Declaration of Independence, influenced the deliberations of the Constitutional Convention, articulated a sense of providence like the one that touched Abraham Lincoln, and instructed the children, grandchildren, and great-great grandchildren of his initial American readers on the virtues of the English common law.'[163] Blackstone's *Commentaries* remained for more than a century 'the basis of US legal education, moulding American legal thought and practice throughout the nineteenth century and beyond.'[164] Indeed, 'the great majority of [American] lawyers continued until the twentieth century to learn their law from Blackstone'[165], who taught that 'the law of nature ... dictated by God himself ... is binding ... in all countries and all times; no human laws are of any validity, if contrary to this; and such of them as are valid derive all their force and all their authority, mediately or immediately, from its original'.[166]

---

[162] Kirk, above n.56, p 145.
[163] Albert W. Alschuler, 'Rediscovering Blackstone' (1996) 145 *University of Pennsylvania Law Review* 1, p 2
[164] Ibid.
[165] Berman, above n.111, p 4.
[166] William Blackstone, *Commentaries on the Laws of England* (1765-1769), Ch 2.

17

The Faith of the American Founders

The vast majority of the American Founders who signed the Declaration of Independence, who attended the Constitutional Convention, and who framed the First Amendment to the U.S. Constitution, agreed that both morality and religion are the 'bedrocks of a stable society'. They believed that education, morality and religion went hand in hand,[167] so they expressed the general belief that 'Providence' had a special plan for the early Republic. These American revolutionaries, writes Martin E. Marty, 'proclaimed that the British were enslaving them by depraving them of representation in policies that affected them all, and that it was their sacred duty to rebel against such slavery. Just as they expected citizens to lay their lives on the line in the war, so they also stressed the need for virtue and morality, ordinarily based on or related to religion.'[168]

This is why the American Founders were so keen to enact the Northwest Ordinance in 1787, a statute which declared that 'Religion, morality and knowledge, being necessary to good government and the happiness of mankind, Schools and the

---

[167] Brion McClanahan, *The Founding Fathers' Guide to the Constitution*, Washington/DC: Regnery Publishing, 2012, p 184.

[168] Martin E. Marty, 'The American Revolution and Religion 1765-1815', *in* Stewart J. Brown and Timothy Tackett (eds.), *Christianity: Enlightenment, Reawakening and Revolution 1660-1815* (Cambridge University Press, 2006), p 499

means of education, shall forever be encouraged.'[169] In George Washington's famous 1796 Farewell Address he expressed the widespread conviction that religion, morality and good government are fundamentally intertwined so that morality can never be maintained without religious sentiment. 'Of all the dispositions and habits which lead to political prosperity', President Washington declared,

> religion and morality are indispensable supports. In vain would that man claim the tribute of patriotism, who should labor to subvert these great pillars of human happiness, these firmest props of the duties of men and citizens. The mere politician, equally with the pious man, ought to respect and to cherish them. A volume could not trace all their connections with private and public felicity. Let it simply be asked: Where is the security for property, for reputation, for life, if the sense of religious obligation deserts the oaths which are the instruments of investigation in courts of justice? And let us with caution indulge the supposition that morality can be maintained without religion. Whatever may be conceded to the influence of refined education on minds of peculiar structure, reason and experience both forbid us to expect that national morality can prevail in exclusion of religious principle.

Naturally, when Washington and the other Founding Fathers highlighted the importance of religion for society, they were not talking about every religion *per se*. While the Founders constantly referred to religion as a positive force in terms of social development and personal freedom, they primarily thought of religion as a Judeo-Christian religion. For example, Patrick Henry (1736-1799) – who is famous for the cry, 'Give me

---

[169] Quoted in Johnson, above n.17, p 209.

84

liberty or give me death' – made this remarkable statement: 'It cannot be emphasized too strongly or too often that this great nation was founded, not by religionists, but by Christians; not only religions, but on the Gospel of Jesus Christ.'

The American Founders were particularly sceptical of the social benefits of the Islamic religion. Benjamin Franklin's *Poor Richard* wonders: 'It is worse to follow Mahomet than the Devil?' This was a rhetorical question. Franklin and most of the Founders thought they actually knew the answer: 'to follow the former meant following the latter.'[170] Indeed, the Founders manifested very serious reservations about any social benefits of the Islamic faith. To put it mildly, they did not hold Islam in a high esteem and often associated the Muslim nations with the world's worst examples of barbarism, tyranny and oppression that in themselves magnified the threat they meant to fight. According to Thomas S. Kidd, 'defenders of the Revolutionary ideas pointed regularly to Muslim states as models of tyranny that crushed essential freedoms.' In sum, the Founders interpreted Islam as a tyrannical religion that promoted irrational ideas about law and society that often required official backing of the State to survive.[171]

Curiously, one of the leading arguments against the establishment of an official religion in the United States was precisely that this would be more appropriate for an Islamic nation, rather than a Christian nation since 'Mahomet called in the use of law and sword to convert people to his religion; but

---

[170] Thomas S. Kidd, 'The Founders and Islam', *in* Daniel L. Dreisbach and Mark David Hall (eds.), *Faith and the Founders of the American Republic* (New York/NY: Oxford University Press, 2014), p 84
[171] Ibid, p 85.

Jesus did not, does not.'[172] This anti-Islamic sentiment did not diminish during the post-Revolutionary era but intensified due to the renewal of Muslim piracy in the Mediterranean. In 1786 John Adams and Thomas Jefferson attempted to negotiate an agreement with the envoy of the Sultan of Tripoli. The envoy's reply, as recorded by Jefferson, fulfilled the Americans' worst suspicions about the religious motivations of the Islamic states:

> The Ambassador answered us that it was founded on the Laws of their Prophet, that it was written in their Koran, that all nations who should not have acknowledged their authority were sinners, that it was their right and duty to make war upon them wherever they could be found, and to make slaves of all they could take as Prisoners, and that every [Muslim] who should be slain in battle was sure to go to Paradise.[173]

To the extent that the religion of Islam was a part of early American history, it was unquestionably a negative force, clearly an external enemy. Therefore, any claim that Islam was part of the American Founding history is nothing but a historical fabrication. For instance, John Quincy Adams (1767-1848) 'regarded Islam, and Muhammad, with horror'.[174] He helped Jefferson compose the Declaration of Independence, and he helped negotiate the Treaty of Paris (1783) that ended the Revolutionary War. He then served as President Washington's Vice President for two terms, and then, as his successor, as the country's sixth President. Above all, he was the greatest defender, in his day, both of Indian rights and of African slaves. And yet, according to Hugh Fitzgerald,

---

[172] Ibid, p 87.
[173] Ibid, p 85
[174] Hugh Fitzgerald, 'John Quincy Adams: Steady, Active, and Industrious' (Part I)', Jihad Watch, July 15, 2017.

'his denunciation of Islam does not contradict, but rather, is consonant with those views, and springs from the same sources of moral indignation'.[175]

In 1841, J.Q. Adams defended 53 Africans accused of mutiny aboard the ship *Amistad*. African slaves were purchased at Muslim slave markets. He won their case before the Supreme Court, giving them back liberty. His opinion about Islam and Muslim behaviour is found in 'Essay on Turks' (The American Annual Register for 1827-28-29): 'The natural hatred of the Mussulmen towards the infidels is in just accordance with the precepts of the Koran... Such is the spirit, which governs the hearts of men, to whom treachery and violence are taught as principles of religion', he wrote. Adams continued:

> In the 7th century of the Christian era, a wandering Arab ... spread desolation and delusion over an extensive portion of the earth. ... He declared undistinguishing and exterminating war as a part of his religion. ... The essence of his doctrine was violence and lust, to exalt the brutal over the spiritual part of human nature.[176]

A similar opinion is provided in 'The Annotated John Quincy Adams – A Bibliography' (1830):

> The vanquished may purchase their lives, by the payment of tribute; the victorious may be appeased by a false and delusive promise of peace. ... The faithful follower of the prophet may submit to the imperious necessities of defeat: but the command to propagate the Moslem creed by the sword is always obligatory, when it can be made effective. The commands of the prophet may be performed alike, by fraud, or by force.[177]

---

[175] Ibid.
[176] Bill Federer, 'How John Quincy Adams Felt About Muslims', WorldDaily-Net, at February 20, 2017.
[177] Ibid.

John Quincy Adams believed that the 'fundamental doctrine of the Christian religion is the extirpation of hatred from the human heart. It forbids the exercise of it, even towards enemies'.[178] As diplomat, lawyer, congressman, and President, he woke every day at 5 am to walk four miles and then read several books of the Bible, usually in English, but often, too, in Greek, or French.[179] His correspondences to his son are compiled in 'Letters of John Quincy Adams to his son, on the Bible and its Teachings'. It contains, among other equally remarkable passages, the following statement: 'No book in the world deserves to be so unceasingly studied, and so profoundly meditated upon as the Bible.'[180] From St. Petersburg in Russia, he also wrote to his son, in September 1811:

> My dear Son, You mentioned that you read to your aunt a chapter in the Bible or a section of Doddridge's Annotations every evening. This information gave me real pleasure; for so great is my veneration for the Bible. [...] It is of all books in the world, that which contributes most to make men good, wise, and happy. My custom is, to read four to five chapters every morning immediately after rising from my bed. [...] It is essential, my son [...] that you should form and adopt certain rules of your own conduct. It is in the Bible, you must learn them. [...] 'Thou shalt love the Lord thy God, with all thy heart, and with all thy soul, and with all thy mind, and with all thy strength, and thy neighbor as thy self.' On these two commandments, Jesus Christ expressly says, 'hang all the law and the prophets'.[181]

---

[178] 'The Annotated John Quincy Adams – A Bibliography,' compiled by Lynn H. Parsons (Westport, CT, 1993, p. 41, entry#194)
[179] Fitzgerald, above n.175.
[180] Federer, above n.177.
[181] Ibid.

17.1. Benjamin Franklin: 'The First American'

Benjamin Franklin earned the deserving title of 'The First American' for his early and indefatigable campaigning for colonial unity and, afterwards, for American Independence. Among all the American Founders he is the only who can be fairly described as a Deist. In his youth Franklin was outspoken about his Deism, writing even a tract which denied the immortality of the soul and God's intervention in the course of human affairs. But as Franklin matured he gradually started to realise that God intervened more directly in the affairs of individuals and nations through 'special providences'; so that, in the early 1750s '[h]e came to see the publication of his Deist tract and its radical tenets as one of the great errors of his youth, particularly when he considered the immoral behaviour it seemed to provoke in himself and his fellow freethinking comrades.'[182] From that moment on Franklin decided to promote actively the advancement of the Christian religion.

Perhaps not so known is that Franklin authored an abridged version of the 'Book of Common Prayer'. The version he drafted contains a form of religious service whose climax is the singing of Milton's 'Hymn to the Creator'. Franklin was convinced that Christian values work as a fundamental hindrance to anti-social, immoral behaviour. And he famously rebuked Thomas Paine for readily dismissing the Christian religion as 'needless'. 'He who spits in the wind spits in his own face ... If men are wicked

---

[182] Benjamin Franklin, Autobiography, 73-74. Quoted in Darren Staloff, 'Deism and the Founders', in Daniel L. Dreisbach and Mark David Hall (eds.), *Faith and the Founders of the American Republic* (New York/NY: Oxford University Press, 2014), p 26.

with religion, what would they be without it?', he asked.[183]

Franklin believed in a God of Reason and Law who holds human responsible for his or her individual actions. 'They could do good or evil, and would be rewarded or punished in this life or in a life to come.'[184] In 1787, when the Constitutional Convention was on the verge of breaking up, Franklin personally called his fellow delegates for a special moment of joint prayer. In his most famous speech he pleaded them to request the assistance of God, because the new nation needed him to be her friend, not her enemy. This is what Franklin said:

> Do we imagine we no longer need His assistance? ...I have lived, Sir, a long time; and the longer I live, the more convincing proofs I see of this truth: that God governs in the affairs of men. And if a sparrow cannot fall to the ground without His notice, it is probable that an empire can rise without His aid?[185]

17.2. George Washington: 'The Greatest of all Founding Fathers'

George Washington was undeniably the most influential of all the American Founding Fathers. The great-great grandfather of Lawrence Washington – an Anglican minister whose son John had migrated to America in 1656 – the young Washington was raised in a deeply devout Christian family. His mother habitually read the Holy Bible for him and his siblings, which reportedly led Washington to memorize entire passages from

---

[183] Rene Williamson, Independence and Involvement (Baton Rouge, 1964), i 131. Quoted in Johnson, above n.17, p 208.
[184] Marty, above n.168, p 507.
[185] John Eidsmoe, above n.23, p 208.

scripture.[186] By the age of twenty-three he credited to God's providence the fact that he had already survived deadly smallpox, Indian ambushes, a near drowning, and a disastrous battle with the French. This led Washington to believe that God had spared his life for a purpose; that God had a special plan for him in the life of the new nation.

Washington routinely recorded what he perceived as the work of God in his life.[187] Writing to his brother, he believed that he 'now exist[s] and appear[s] in the land of the living by the miraculous care of Providence that protected [him] beyond all human expectation.'[188] In adulthood he began to collect sermons and to fast regularly. On 1 June 1774, Washington penned in his diary: 'Went to church and fasted all day.'[189] Not only did he become an active church leader, but Washington always carried with him a copy of the book of Psalms. What is more, in his personal letters he constantly made references to his lifelong belief that God had repeatedly and miraculously intervened in his life and in the life of the new nation – what he described the 'astonishing interpositions of Providence'.[190] The reference to Providence is a common theme in Washington's writings and correspondences. Far from advocating separation between church and state, these letters reveal that the greatest of all the Founding Fathers 'consistently sought to use governmental authority to encourage religion and to foster the religious

---

[186] Gragg, above n.18, p 19.
[187] Ibid, p 20.
[188] Ibid, p 24.
[189] George Washington, 'Diaries of George Washington', 3: 254-55. Quoted from Gragg, above n.18, p 34.
[190] Gragg, above n.18, p 27.

character of the American people.'[191]

When the Continental Congress appointed Washington as the Commander-in-Chief, 'of all the continental forces raised or to be raised for the defence of American liberty', his first measure on 15 June 1775 urged the officers under his command to encourage a 'true Christian spirit' among the troops.[192] Later on he issued personal orders encouraging the troops to attend Sunday worship services in camp. Further, Washington forbade military reviews on Sundays because this is commonly regarded as 'the Lord's Day'. Above all, Washington asked the Continental army to display the 'Character of a Christian',[193] urging each of the soldiers to behave as 'a Christian soldier defending the dearest Rights and Liberties of his country.'[194]

Throughout the revolutionary war Washington expressed a strong conviction that 'the hand of Providence' would ultimately determine America's future. He even issued a general order to remind that the 'blessings and protection of Heaven are at all times necessary, but especially in times of distress and dangers.'[195] Thus as the country's first President Washington inaugurated the 'Thanksgiving Day' – a holiday Americans deeply cherish to this present day. President Washington declared:

> It is the duty of all nations to acknowledge the providence of Almighty God, to obey His will, to be grateful for His
> · mercy, to implore His protection and favor ... That great and glorious Being who is the beneficent author of all the

---

[191] Vincent Phillip Muñoz, *God and Founders: Madison, Washington, and Jefferson* (New York/NY: Cambridge University Press, 2009), p 50.
[192] Gragg, above n.18, p 33.
[193] General Orders, 5 October, 1777, GWP. Quoted from Gragg, above n.18, p 55.
[194] Ibid, p 63.
[195] Ibid.

good that was, that is, or that ever will be, that we may then unite in rendering unto Him and humble thanks for His kind care and protection of the people.[196]

This is a theme Washington frequently evoked during his presidency. He sincerely hoped that the American people would never forget what God had done for them during the War of Independence. Above all, he held a very strong conviction that God had miraculously intervened to rescue the American cause from imminent defeat.[197] Hence Washington stated at his inaugural address as the first President of the United States:

> I am sure there never was a people who had more reason to acknowledge a divine interposition in their affairs, then those of the United States'. 'And I should be pained to believe that they have ... failed to consider the omnipotence of that God who is alone above to protect them.[198]

Evidently, Washington's personal character and actions were firmly rooted in a Christian philosophy. During his political life he repeatedly referred to God as the great lawgiver and expressed the belief that, as Washington put it, '[i]t is the duty of all Nations to acknowledge the providence of Almighty God.'[199] Like most of the Founding Fathers, he weighed everything in accordance with Christian values and principles – especially the activities of the American government – thus expressing a commitment to the concept of natural law and its correlating idea of God-given inalienable rights, which, of course, are fully encapsulated in the Declaration of Independence.

---

[196] J D Richardson (ed.), Compilation of the Messages and Papers of the Presidents, 1789-1797, 10 vols. (New York, 1969), i 64. Quoted in Johnson, above n.15, p 211.
[197] Gragg, above n.18, p 1.
[198] Ibid
[199] Ibid, p 54.

17.3. Thomas Jefferson: 'The Drafter of the Declaration of Independence'

Thomas Jefferson was the main drafter of the Declaration of Independence. He was also the nation's third President. Jefferson has been regarded as the least of all the Founding Fathers affected by biblical Christianity. Some authors even describe him as an atheist, which, of course, is completely false. Although it is true that Jefferson opposed attempts to allow the Virginian legislature to subsidize the local churches, nothing in his writings reveal a hostility to religion. What Jefferson disliked the most was not religiosity per se, but the 'intolerance and any restriction of religious practice by those who would not admit the legitimacy of diverse beliefs.'[200] Jefferson's *Bill for Establishing Religious Freedom*, which is justified in its own preamble, is based on the premise that coercion of belief was not in accord with God's plan.[201] Thus he drafted such a bill in 1777, which the State Assembly enacted in January 1786, that is considered a precursor of the Establishment Clause and Free Exercise Clause of the First Amendment to the United States Constitution.

Jefferson was not anti-religious; he was simply against the establishment of a national church. He was vehemently opposed to any state church that imposes religious conformity. He also opposed any governmental favour of one church over another. However, Jefferson constantly wrote about 'providence' and 'inalienable rights', which the American

---

[200] Johnson, above n.17, p 207.
[201] See: Thomas Jefferson, *A Bill for Establishing Religious Freedom* (1785), reprinted in Adams and Emmerich, A Nation Dedicated to Religious Liberty, p.110. See also: Cord, Separation of Church and State, pp 36-46.

94

Declaration so fully testifies.[202] Jefferson's faith even led him to compile a redaction of the moral teachings of Jesus Christ. Above all, Jefferson 'believed that he was a Christian and one of the few who truly understood the teachings of its founder.'[203]

In his 1801 Inaugural Address as President of the United States, Jefferson praised the nation's 'benign religion, professed, indeed, and practiced in various forms, yet all of them inculcating honesty, truth, temperance, gratitude, and the love of man; acknowledging and adoring an overruling Providence, which by all its dispensations proves that it delights in the happiness of man here and his greater happiness thereafter.'[204] Engraved on a wall inside the Jefferson Memorial in Washington D.C. is Jefferson's statement:

> God who gave us life gave us liberty. Can the liberties of a nation be thought secure when we have removed their only firm basis, a conviction in the minds of the people that these liberties are the gift of God? That they are not to be violated but with his wrath? Indeed I tremble for my country when I reflect that God is just: that his justice

---

[202] As Jefferson once confided to John Adams, in 1816: 'I think it is a good world on the whole, and framed on Principles of Benevolence, and more pleasure than pain dealt out to us'. – L J Cappon (ed.), The Adams-Jefferson Letters, 2 vols. (Chapel Hill, 1959), ii, p 467. Quoted in Johnson, above n.15, p 207.

[203] Staloff, above n.182, p 25.

[204] *The First Inaugural Address of President Thomas Jefferson, Washington, March 4, 1801. Available at: http://www.freedomshrine.com/documents/jefferson.html*

cannot sleep forever.[205]

This remarkable statement reveals Jefferson's strong conviction that, although enshrined in the Bill of Rights, the most fundamental rights of the individual are ultimately a 'gift of God'. Also implicit in such statement is the view that the nation may draw God's wrath if these liberties – given as a great gift by God – are misused, infringed, abused, encroached upon or not respected. After his presidency, Jefferson proposed that students of the newly created University of Virginia should be required to study '[t]he proofs of the being of a God, the creator, preserver and supreme ruler, the author of all relations within morality, and of the laws and obligations these infer.'[206]

---

[205] This statement comes from two different writings by Jefferson. In both works he makes it clear that he believed our liberty comes from God. The two original Jefferson quotes in their entirety: 'For in a warm climate, no man will labour for himself who can make another labour for him. This is so true, that of the proprietors of slaves a very small proportion indeed are ever seen to labor. And can the liberties of a nation be thought secure when we have removed their only firm basis, a conviction in the minds of the people that these liberties are the gift of God? That they are not to be violated but with his wrath? Indeed I tremble for my country when I reflect that God is just: that his justice cannot sleep for ever . . . .' – Thomas Jefferson, in Notes on the State of Virginia.

'But let them [members of the parliament of Great Britain] not think to exclude us from going to other markets to dispose of those commodities which they cannot use, or to supply those wants which they cannot supply. Still less let it be proposed that our properties within our own territories shall be taxed or regulated by any power on earth but our own. The God who gave us life gave us liberty at the same time; the hand of force may destroy, but cannot disjoin them.' –Thomas Jefferson, in A Summary View of the Rights of British America

[206] Quoted in Herbert Adams, *Thomas Jefferson and the University of Virginia* (Washington/DC: Government Printing Office, 1888), p 91.

17.4. Alexander Hamilton: 'The Architect of the Constitution'

Alexander Hamilton is widely regarded as the principal architect of the Constitution. Noticeably devout in his youth, he was a committed Christian during his college years. Although he appears to have become less committed to the Christian faith in his adulthood, there are no instances in Hamilton's voluminous writings or correspondences of him ever criticising Scripture, or expressing anti-Christian sentiments. Later in his life, particularly after the death of his son Phillip, Hamilton became deeply religious, not only regularly leading his family in prayer and devotion but also organising a national 'Christian Constitutional Society'.[207] In spring 1787 Hamilton wrote:

> The sacred rights of mankind are not to be rummaged for amongst old parchments or musty records. They are written, as with a sunbeam, in the whole volume of human nature by the hand of Divinity itself, and can never be erased or obscured by mortal power.[208]

17.5. James Madison: 'The Drafter of the Constitution'

Because James Madison was so instrumental in the drafting of the United States' Constitution, he is deservedly hailed as the "Father of the Constitution". Curiously, Madison's political writings are dotted with theological points as well as notes on Scripture.[209] The Scottish Presbyterian minister, Donald Robertson, educated Madison in his early years. Consequently, Madison was positively pious and once he spent the entire year

---

[207] Staloff, above n.182, p 22.
[208] James Avery Joyce, *The New Politics of Human Rights* (Macmillan, 1978), p. 7.
[209] Johnson, above n.15, 207.

just reading theology books after graduation from Princeton. About the impact of Reverend Robertson on his personal life and political philosophy, Madison stated: 'All that I have been in life I owe largely to that man.'[210] Consistent with his Christian worldview, when he became the fourth President of the United States, Madison urged Congress to enact public days of prayer and thanksgiving. As the chief architect of the written constitution, he famously declared:

> We have staked the whole future of American civilization, not on the power of government, far from it. We have staked the future of all of our political institutions upon the capacity of each and all of us to govern ourselves ... according to the Ten Commandments of God.[211]

Throughout his successful political career, Madison did not produce a single word in opposition to Christian doctrine or revelation. Although his Memorial and Remonstrance (written in 1785 in a successful effort to defeat Patrick Henry's bill to support all churches in Virginia) is often cited as justifying the separation of church and state, such is actually a religious document, not a secular one. The Memorial's often quoted statement that 'the opinions of men, depending only on the evidence contemplated by their own minds, cannot follow the dictates of other men', is actually a defence of the right to hold one's own religion. Madison thought that one's obligation to God is prior to his subsidiary obligation to the secular government, which meant that ultimately the state is subordinate to God. Professor Carter explains:

> The point is that the Memorial and Remonstrance,

---

[210] Staloff, above n.184, 25.
[211] David Barton, The Myth of Separation: What Is the Correct Relationship Between Church and State? (5th Ed., Wallbuilder Press, 1992), p 120.

although it plainly defends the separation of church and state, frames the argument principally as a protection of the church, not as a protection of the state. Indeed, the entire disestablishment movement in Virginia was a movement to rescue religious freedom from state oppression, not to rescue the state from religious oppression.[212]

17.6. John Adams: 'Principal Leader of the American Independence'

John Adams was the principal leader of the American independence. He followed George Washington as the second President of the United States (1797-1801). Adams regarded the 'general principles of Christianity' every bit 'as eternal and immutable as the Existence and Attributes of God.'[213] In his youth, Adams, a descendant of the Puritans, contemplated becoming a Christian minister. Although changing his mind, he never changed his opinion on the need of religion for the preservation of public morality. To the contrary, Adams was adamant that the nation's entire constitutional experiment was heavily dependent for its regular functioning on the Judeo-Christian foundations of law and morality. In Spring 1789, Adams stated: 'Our Constitution was made only for a moral and religious people. It is wholly inadequate for the government of any other.'[214] Speaking later with the authority of American President, Adams declared:

> One great advantage of the Christian religion is that it

---

[212] Stephen L. Carter, *The Culture of Disbelief: How American Law and Politics Trivialise Religious Devotion* (New York/NY: Anchor Books, 1994), p 116.

[213] Letter of John Adams to Thomas Jefferson, June 28, 1813. Quoted from Staloff, above n.182, p 25.

[214] Cited by A. James Reichley, *Religion in American Public Life* (Washington/DC: Brookings Press, 1985), p 105

brings the great principle of the law of nature and nations, love your neighbour as yourself, and do to others as you would others should do to you – to the knowledge, belief and veneration of the whole people. Children, servants, women as well as men are all professors in the science of public as well as private morality ... The duties and rights of the citizen are thus taught from early infancy to every creature'.[215]

Adams held the Jewish people and their religion in the highest esteem. Such an appreciation for Judaism – and the contribution of Jews to the making of a better world – is most evident in his private letters sent to close friends. In the whole of his political writings, Adams drew heavily on Greek and Roman political experience but did not ignore the patrimony of the Hebrews. He wrote in 1809:

> I will insist that the Hebrews have done more to civilize men than any other nation. If I were an atheist, and believed in blind eternal fate, I should still believe that fate had ordained the Jews to be the most essential instrument for civilizing the nations. If I were an atheist of the other sect, who believe or pretend to believe that all is ordered by chance, I should believe that chance had ordered the Jews to preserve and propagate to all mankind the doctrine of a supreme, intelligent, wise, almighty sovereign of the universe, which I believe to be the great essential principle of all morality, and consequently of all civilization.[216]

---

[215] John Adams also wrote on his Abigail when the American Declaration of Independence was signed: 'The second day of July 1776 will be the most memorable epoch in the history of America ... it will be celebrated by succeeding generations as a great anniversary festival. It ought to be commemorated as the day of deliverance, by solemn acts of devotion to God Almighty.' Quoted in Johnson, above n 19, p 208.

[216] Letter of John Adams to F.A. Vanderkemp, February 16, 1809, in C. F. Adams (ed.), *The Works of John Adams* (Boston: Little, Brown, 1854), Vol. IX, pp. 609-10.

President Adams is on record supporting not only the re-creation of the nation of Israel, but also the full return of the Jewish people to their 'promised land'.[217] In a missive dated December 31, 1808, he confessed being appalled by Voltaire's derogatory comments about the Hebrew Bible and the Jewish people. Adams commented:

> How is it possible this old Fellow [Voltaire] should represent the Hebrews in such contemptible light?, They are the most glorious Nation that ever inhabited this Earth. The Romans and their Empire were but a Bauble in comparison of the Jews. They have given Religious to the quarters of the globe and have influenced the affairs of mankind more, and more happily than any other Nation ancient or modern.[218]

---

[217] Dalin, above n. 73, p 73.
[218] John Adams to F.A. Van Der Kemp, February 6, 1809, quoted in Dalin, above n.73, p 72.

18

The U.S. Declaration of Independence

Christian beliefs throughout history have been largely responsible for persuading governments to place greater value on individual rights, personal freedom, freedom of religion, equality before the law, and separation of church and state.[219] Christianity provided the intellectual background leading to the cultural values that are still held by many Americans today, including legal protection of individual rights; the respect for personal freedom; and the respect for the rule of law. Such an influence can be traced directly to the Declaration of Independence. As Wayne Grudem points out,

> The biblical teaching that all human beings are created in the image of God and therefore have equal status before God had a significant influence on the thinking of the Founding Fathers of the United States and their bold declaration that 'all men are created equal'. This stood in clear contrast to the prior assumption in many European nations that there was a special group of human beings known as 'royalty' who had the hereditary right to rule over ordinary people.[220]

---

[219] See Alvin Schmidt, *How Christianity Changed the World* (Grand Rapids/MI: Zondervan, 2004).
[220] Wayne Grudem, *Politics According to the Bible* (Grand Rapids/MI: Zondervan, 2010), p.63.

It was a congressional committee comprised of Thomas Jefferson, Benjamin Franklin, Roger Sherman, John Adams, and Robert Livingstone which drafted the American Declaration of Independence. This document uses Lockean overtones in order to justify, first, uniting the colonies of America and, second, that these united colonies were entitled to full independence by the 'Laws of Nature and of Nature's God'. According to Eidsmoe, the Declaration reveals the Founders' belief in a Creator who 'was more than the impersonal and uninvolved god of the deists; the term providence implies a God who continually provides for the human race.'[221] This role of the Christian religion was incredibly important and it reveals the belief in 'a Provident God would bless their efforts, ennoble their sacrifices, and bless their beginnings as a new nation.'[222] In 1776, a national seal was conceived which included the Latin slogan 'Annuit Coepits' – the Divine has 'blessed our beginnings.' The Declaration even closes with a final appeal to the 'Supreme Judge of the world for the rectitude of [their] intentions', and the 'firm reliance on the protection of Divine Providence', and so pledging their 'lives, their fortunes, and their sacred honor'. As noted by Martin E. Marty,

> The religion of the American Revolution … implied what we might call a metaphysical background, a sense or claim that behind ordinary appearances of national life

---

[221] John Eidsmoe, 'Operation Josiah: Rediscovering the Biblical Roots', in H Wayne House (ed), *The Christian and American Law : Christianity's Impact on America's Founding Documents and Future Direction* (Grand Rapids/MI: Kregel Publications, 1998) 91; Blackstone's *Commentaries on the Laws of England* was a huge success in the Americas – for many, it was their first comprehensive and clear insight into the English legal system and it was this example which many future American lawmakers modelled their laws upon.

[222] Marty, above n.168, p 506.

there existed a larger narrative and set of meanings and expectations. Thus Thomas Jefferson and his colleagues in the Declaration of Independence made the religious claim that their rights were 'endowed by their Creator'. George Washington and other military and constitutional leaders joined Jefferson in speaking of 'Nature's God' unconfined by a particular set of scriptures. They invoked 'Providence' and 'Heaven' to guide them in battle and in drafting documents for the new nation.[223]

The English word "declaration" comes from the French *déclaration*. In France, prior to the French Revolution of 1789, the word often pertained to the public statements of the king. In England, by contrast, when the subjects wanted a reaffirmation of their rights, they drew up their own declarations. Thus, the Magna Carta of 1215 formalized the rights of Englishmen in relation to their king; the Petition of Right of 1628 confirmed the "diverse Rights and Liberties of the Subjects"; and the English Bill of Rights of 1689 validated "the true, ancient and indubitable rights and liberties of the people of this kingdom".[224]

In 1776's America, the words "charter", "petition", and "bill" seemed inadequate to the task of guaranteeing rights. "Petition" and "bill" both implied a request or appeal to the monarch as the political sovereign, and "charter" often meant an old document or deed. As noted by Lynn Hunt, 'Declaration had less of a musty, submissive air. Moreover, unlike "petition", or even "charter", "declaration" could signify the intent to seize sovereignty'.[225] In this context, Jefferson began the Declaration of Independence with an explanation of the need to proclaim

---

[223] Ibid., p 499.
[224] Lynn Hunt, *Inventing Human Rights: A History* (New York/NY: W.W. Norton & Co., 2007), p 114.
[225] Ibid., p 115.

it: 'When in the course of human events, it becomes necessary for one people to dissolve the political bands which have connected them with another, and to assume among the powers of the earth, the separate and equal station to which the Laws of Nature and of Nature's God entitle them, a decent respect to the opinion of mankind requires that they should declare the causes which impel them to the separation'. Such an expression of "decent respect" does not obscure the main purpose: that the colonies were 'declaring themselves a separate and equal state and seizing their own sovereignty'.[226]

The core belief manifested in the Declaration of Independence is that 'all men are created equal and that they are endowed by God with inalienable rights'. This statement can be traced directly to the Christian tradition of natural law. By the proposition that all men (and women) are created equal, its authors 'did not mean to say all were equal in color, size, intellect, moral developments, or social capacity'.[227] Rather, as Abraham Lincoln pointed out, that proposition referred to the axiom that we are all members of the same race and created in the image of God. We are all beings capable of understanding reasons over matters of right and wrong. This concept rests on the biblical teaching of the moral law that is written in our hearts, with our conscience bearing witness and accusing us

---

[226] Ibid.

[227] Abraham Lincoln, 'Speech in Chicago', July 10, 1858, *in* Roy P. Basler (ed.), *The Collected Works of Abraham Lincoln* (News Brunswick/NJ: Rutgers University Press, 1953), vol. II, p 499.

whenever we do not act to such a law.[228] Harry Jaffa provides, with remarkable illumination, a good explanation of what the idea that 'all men are created equal' effectively means:

> No man is by nature the ruler of other men in the way that God is by nature the ruler of men, and men are by nature the ruler of horses and dogs. And, therefore, as the argument ran, if we find about us today a situation in which some men are put in the position of ruling over others, that state of affairs cannot arise from nature. It must arise from convention or consent.[229]

The Declaration of Independence speaks of "self-evident truths" and "certain unalienable rights." As noted by Robert A Sirico, such a view is 'an inheritance which is carved into the very foundations of Judeo-Christian culture'.[230] He explains that the idea of personal freedom was fully born in European Christendom because the Judeo-Christian tradition underlines not only the truth of humanity's material dimension, but also that we are not merely the dust of the earth; we are 'vivified by the breath of life'. Such a transcendence is at the root of human

---

[228] Romans 2: 12-16. I find this theological explanation of Romans 2:12-15 particularly helpful: 'If you travelled around the world, you would find evidence in every society and culture of God's moral law. For example, all cultures prohibit murder, and yet in all societies that law has been broken. We belong to a stubborn race. We know what's right but we insist on doing what's wrong. It is not enough to know what's right; we must also do it. Admit to yourself and to God that you fit the human pattern and frequently fail to live up to your own standards (much more to God's standards). That's the first step to forgiveness and healing'. – *Life Application Study Bible: New King James Version* (Carol Stream/IL: Tyndale House Publishing, 1996), p 2058.

[229] Harry V. Jaffa, Equality and Liberty (Claremont, 1999), pp 177-8. Quoted from Hadley Arkes, *Natural Rights and the Right to Choose* (New York/NY: Cambridge University Press, 2002) p 45.

[230] The Reverend Robert Sirico, 'How Will Freedom Succeed?', *Robert H. Krieble lecture delivered on April 24, 2008, at the 31st annual meeting of The Heritage Foundation Resource Bank in Atlanta/GO.*

rights and dignity because it raises humans above all the other animals, thus making us fully 'capable of infinite creativity to resolve the challenges of our fragile existence'.[231] Indeed, every member of the human race is considered to be divinely appointed bearers or receivers of 'an eternal dignity', with the Holy Scripture revealing that we have 'an immortal destiny beyond this world'.[232]

There is no need to remind that Lockean theory was particularly influential during the draft of the American Declaration. John Locke believed in 'natural rights' and the right to resist governments that violate these rights. Locke's anthropology is built upon his Christian views, and such views are essential to his more substantial contributions in political theory. Accordingly, his writings on religion were an important aspect of his productive life. Remarkably, the assertion in the Declaration that 'all men are created equal' is also argued by Locke in the same cast in his *Second Treatise on Civil Government*:

> For men being all the workmanship of one ... wise Maker ..., and being furnished with like faculties, sharing all in one community of nature, there cannot be supposed any such subordination among us that may authorize us to destroy one another, as if we were made for one another's uses, as the inferior ranks of creatures are for ours.[233]

Dyson Heydon, a former High Court judge in Australia, once commented that modern liberalism is actually the product of a long historical process that arouse out of Christianity. According to Heydon, 'liberalism in any genuine sense rests on a belief

---

[231] Ibid.
[232] Ibid.
[233] John Locke, 'Second Treatise on Civil Government', Bk.I, Ch. II, in Sir Ernst Baker (ed.) *Social Contract* (Oxford/UK: Oxford University Press, 1960), pp 5-6.

in individual liberty, in the moral equality of individuals, in a legal system based on equal treatment of like cases, and in a representative form of democratic government'. Such values are derived from the revolutionary teachings of Christ', he says.[234] As Heydon notes:

> Christ showed a concern for the ill, the socially marginal, the outsider, the destitute. He opposed self-righteousness and hypocrisy. He had no concern to associate with wealth, power or celebrity. His associates were humbler. Many of them were women. He saw little children as heirs to the kingdom of heaven. He encouraged a search for the beam in one's own eye before identifying the mote in someone else's. He encouraged his followers not merely to love their friends and neighbours but also to forgive their enemies. He urged them not to meet violence with violence. His social teachings were reflected, for example, in the monastic tradition later. Thus in the fourth century, St Basil of Caesarea said: "it is God's will that we should nourish the hungry, give the thirsty to drink, and clothe the naked". They live on in religious charities even to this day. But above all Christ taught that all human beings were equal before God, and all could enter the kingdom of God.[235]

The apostle Paul told the Galatians: 'There is neither Jew nor Greek, there is neither bond nor freed, there is neither male

---

[234] As Dyson Hydon points out, *"[h]is followers came to treat his life as a revolutionary and dramatic intervention of the divine into secular affairs. His enemies saw him as a rebel against unsympathetic religious leaders and Jewish puppets of Roman governors. His followers, however, saw him as having universal significance for each individual human being".* – Dyson Heydon, 'Liberalism Built on Christian Principles is Lost on Modern Elites', *The Australian*, November 4, 2017.

[235] Ibid.

not female: for you are all one in Christ Jesus.'[236] Christianity is based on the belief that we are all equal before God and, as such, are born with that the Declaration of Independence describes as 'unalienable rights.[237] Accordingly, governments must respect a cluster of fundamental rights that citizens possess by nature. This is clearly spelled out in the Declaration of Independence.[238] In its own very structure, says Charles J. Chaput,

> the Declaration of Independence has a broad religious resonance. It refers several times to a Creator or Supreme Being. But more importantly, natural law principles shape the whole text... Rooted in the nature law, the Declaration affirms that all nations are subject to a higher authority than their own man-made laws... Civil power answers to a higher authority. If a government ignores that higher authority, the governed have no duty to obey that civil power. Later in the Declaration, the signers argue that the British government has violated the colonists' natural rights to 'life, liberty and the pursuit of happiness'. In claiming their rights, the colonists were doing something historically unprecedented. Yet they were not claiming 'new' rights, but their rights already *inherent in Nature*. The Declaration ... saw human beings as 'endowed by our Creator' with certain rights, and created equal – not equal in ability but equal in dignity as moral agents. In the mind of the founders, all human beings

---

[236] Galatians 3:28 (NKJV). In this passage, says Justice Heydon: *"Paul advocated relying on conscience and good intentions and abandoning the ritual behaviour of the ancient world and the Jews, with its mechanical following of rules and immemorial customs. He urged the exercise of free choise in accepting the gift of grace attained through faith in Christ. Salvation was a matter of personal decision to be resolved between each individual and God. In that sense all were equal. Those equal in the eye of God came to be seen as equal in the eye of the law".* – Ibid.

[237] Kevin Donnelly, *The Culture of Freedom* (Melbourne/Vic: Institute of Public Affairs, 2016), p 44.

[238] Francis J. Beckwith, *Politics for Christians: Statecraft as Soulcraft* (Downers Grove/IL: Illinois, 2010), p 146.

are both subject to the moral law and protected by it.[239]

It is patently clear from a factual analysis of the text that the Founders justified their revolutionary actions on Christian principles, believing that these principles derive directly from God's law. They thought these principles are discoverable by reason and ultimately prescribed the inalienability of 'natural rights' to life, liberty and the pursuit of happiness – rights which are God-given and not bestowed or conferred on people by any government. Rather, these rights are regarded as being conferred by God to all humans, so these rights cannot legitimately be denied.[240] In other words, they believed in a natural moral law that is the foundation of every just government, and that this moral law is best accounted for by the existence of God. Interestingly, writes Francis J. Beckwith, 'this seems a better bulwark against the threat of theocracy (which is feared by some unbelievers) than a government whose principles are unstable because they are based on nothing more than power, stipulation or popular sentiments.' Ironically, Beckwith concludes:

> an atheist is better protected in her rights in a state that is grounded in theism than is a Christian in an atheistic state. Perhaps this is why Dawkins, Hitchens and their atheist colleagues have more political freedom to preach their message in largely Christian America than did Aleksandr Solzhenitsyn and other persecuted Christian in the atheistic regime of the Soviet Union.[241]

Arguably, it might be not possible to coherently discuss the

---

[239] Charles J. Chaput, *Render Unto Caesar: Serving the Nation by Living Our Catholic Beliefs in Political Life* (New York/NY: Image Books, 2008), p 84.
[240] Harold Berman, *Faith and Order: the Reconciliation of Law and Religion) Religion* (Atlanta: Scholars Press, 1993), p 210.
[241] Francis J. Beckwith, *Politics for Christians: Statecraft as Soulcraft*(Downers Grove/IL: Illinois, 2010), p 146.

concept of natural law without revelation provided by the author of that law.[242] By detaching it from its constitutive relationship with God as its author, such a concept may be reduced to a condition of self-realisation and so reason is elevated as the sole criterion of legality and ethical behaviour. The final result might be 'the divinization of subjectivity, the infallible oracle of which is conscience, never to be doubted by anyone or anything'.[243] Without the ultimate appeal to a transcendental lawmaker, human conscience becomes a matter of reason detached from any constitutive relationship with transcendental moral truths. Conscience then becomes a product of subjective moral thoughts and so derived from subjective feelings as to how one proceeds in 'doing good and avoiding evil'. After all, as Charles Rice so properly reminded, the premise that we must 'do good and avoid evil',

> have no necessary and universal reference to the truth concerning the good, but would be linked only with the goodness of the subjective intention. Concrete actions, instead, would depend for their moral qualification on the self-understanding of the individual, which is always culturally and circumstantially determined. In this way, conscience becomes nothing but subjectivity elevated to being the ultimate criterion of action. The fundamental Christian idea that nothing can be opposed to conscience no longer has the original and inalienable meaning that truth can only be imposed in virtue of itself, i.e., in personal interiority.[244]

To a certain degree the idea of natural law needs to be

---

[242] Rice, above n.17, p 181.
[243] Joseph Ratzinger, 'The Problem of Threats to Human Life', Address to Consistory of College of Cardinals, 4 April 1991.
[244] Rice, above n.17, p 343.

transcendental in its provenance to make any proper sense. The French revolutionaries of 1789 sought to remove the transcendental properties of the natural law. They substituted them with an entirely humanist foundation. Such a removal did not advance the natural law, or the rights of the individual for that matter. To the contrary, it did not take so long for the anti-religious Jacobins (who enthroned a woman, some say a prostitute, as the 'Goddess of Reason' at Notre Dame Cathedral) to impose their notorious 'Reign of Terror' across the country. Having initially proposed 'the perfection of reason, the last word of the natural-law tradition', the abandonment of transcendental authority to the natural law ended up generating an extreme form of legal positivism, 'which looked on the words and will of the legislator as the sole basis for the law validity'.[245]

The French Revolution was marked by recurring savagery, chaos, political anarchy, the wanton bloodshed of the infamous 'Reign of Terror' – and a bitter assault on Christianity.[246] Whereas the French Declaration of the Rights of Man frames rights in the altogether rationalist view of the Enlightenment and the

---

[245] J.M. Kelly, *A Short History of Western Legal Theory* (Oxford/UK: Oxford University Press, 1992), p 324.

[246] Gragg, above n.18, p.87. Such observation is made in the context of Gragg's comparison between the American and French revolutions. The entire passage reads as follows: 'The American revolution stood in stark contrast to the French Revolution ... although both events occurred in the same age and among people of European extraction. Unlike the American Revolution, the French Revolution was marked by recurring savagery, chaos, political anarchy, the wanton bloodshed of the infamous 'Reign of Terror' – and a bitter assault on Christianity. In Paris, Notre Dame Cathedral was transformed into an irreverent 'Temple of Reason'. The French clergy were reviled rather than revered. The calendar was changed to erase its connection to Christianity, and blood from countless victims of the guillotine pooled on the pavement of the Place de la Concorde. Ultimately, the French Revolution produced prolonged lawlessness and the rise of authoritarian rule'. – p.87.

Encyclopaedists, the American Declaration of Independence was marked by the influence the Christian religion, thus adhering to the Christian character of human rights and freedoms.[247] Undoubtedly legal philosopher Jeffrie G. Murphy considered such things when he correctly stated:

> The rich moral doctrine of the sacredness, the preciousness, the dignity of persons cannot in fact be utterly detached from the theological context in which it arose and of which it for so long formed an essential part. Values come to us trailing their historical past; and when we attempt to cut all links to that past we risk cutting the life lines on which those values essentially depend. I think that this happens in the case of Kant's attempt — and no doubt any other attempt — to retain all Christian moral values within a totally secular framework. Thus 'All men are created equal and are endowed by their Creator with certain inalienable rights' may be a sentence we must accept in an all or nothing fashion – not one where we can simply carve out what we like and junk the rest.[248]

[247] Jacques Maritain, *Natural Law: Reflections on Theory and Practice*, South Bend/IN, St Augustine's Press, 2001), p 71.
[248] Jeffrie G. Murphy, 'Constitutionalism, Moral Skepticism, and Religious Belief', *in* A. S. Rosenbaum (ed.), *Constitutionalism: The Philosophical Dimension* (New York/NY: Greenwood Press, 1988) pp 245–6.

19

The Constitution of the United States

Drawn up by the Second Continental Congress, between 1776 and 1777, the *Articles of Confederation* formed the first attempted written constitution of the United States.[249] The purpose of those *Articles* was to establish a weak central government based on a confederation among the former colonies just turned into sovereign states. This was deemed imperative due to the continuing conflict with Britain. The British experience made the Founders deeply reluctant to establish a strong centralised government, so the Articles provided only a 'loose confederation of independent states' tethered by a weak central government.[250] Unfortunately, however, the very limited powers afforded to the 'general government' under the Articles made the central government apparently too weak and ultimately ineffective. That being so, the States responded by drawing up a stronger charter in the form of the United States Constitution of 1787.

The prevailing view today is that the United States'

---

[249] Stone, above n.51, p 2.
[250] The centralized government was afforded very limited powers under the Articles of Confederation – the government had no powers to regulate trade and levy taxes as these were left in the domain of the states.

Constitution is a 'secular document', and that Christian philosophy did not have a predominant role in its creation or intended interpretation. Those who oppose the notion of Christianity playing any relevant role in American constitutionalism often contend that its foundations, in particular the works of Montesquieu and Locke, are entirely secular. They also claim that the Constitution appoints the people, not God, as the ultimate sovereign, thus beginning with the phrase 'We the People'. This phrase is commonly viewed as '… a repudiation of older European ideas that governments are established by God and derive their power or authority from God (for example, the divine right of kings).'[251] Further, the insertion of the First Amendment (prohibiting the government from establishing any religion and protecting the free exercise of religion) is often interpreted as an express exclusion of any religious exertion on the affairs of government as well as the interpretation of the United States Constitution. According to one such a commentator, 'at no point does the Constitution exhibit anything less than a fully secular, godless character. The American Constitution was a novel experiment in the creation of a secular government on the basis of popular sovereignty and democratic principles.'[252]

All these views are mistaken and a by-product of historical revisionism. The U.S. Constitution is not a 'secular' document just because it does not explicitly contain a reference to Christianity. Instead, the Founders were concerned about the idea of a church established in some way by the state. After all, many of the peoples in the various colonies were of different

---

[251] Austin Cline, *Godless Constitution: Constitutional Law without Gods or Religion* (2008) About.com.
[252] Ibid.

116

religious, religions that sometimes disagreed strongly with each other, and it was genuine fear on the part of many that the new Constitution would be used to promote a particular denominational religious view, to the exclusion of others, and that this might lead to social unrest. And yet, as Brendan Sweetman reminds, the Founders 'recognized that any Constitution worthy of the name would have to satisfy two conditions: (1) it would have to be ultimately based on God's existence and on God's moral law and (2) it would have to include the core values of freedom, quality, justice and the common good, which many people believed in and had fought and died for.'[253] Sweetman explains:

> The American founders ... develop[ed] what we might call a rational core of religious truths, the values of which could form the basis of a system of government. They could then avoid disputes about higher-order doctrinal differences between religious. On this way, they could take what was rational and good from many different traditions, place it at the heart of the Constitution, and then late insert a clause forbidding the establishment of any particular religion and protecting religious freedom. This would preserve freedom of religion, and avoid public life getting bogged down in petty doctrinal disputes.[254]

The religious philosophy of the Founders is well-known and it has been widely documented. There are countless examples pointing to their faith as the foundation of their vision for the new nation and its constitutional design. Overall, the Founders' support for religion rested basically on the broad assumption of Judeo-Christian values and tradition being essential for morality,

---

[253] Brendan Sweetman, *Why Politics Needs Religion: The Place of Religious Arguments in the Public Square*, (Downers Grove/IL: IVP Academic, 2006), p 152
[254] Ibid., p 153.

and that morality in turn was essential for the functioning of every republican government. For example, Gouverneur Morris of Pennsylvania, who was the main draftsman of the American Constitution, stated:

> There must be religion. When that ligament is torn, society is disjointed and its members perish. The nation is exposed to foreign violence and domestic convulsion. Vicious rulers, chosen by vicious people, turn back the current of corruption to its source. They take bribes. They sell statutes and decrees. They sell honor and office. They sell their conscience. They sell their country. By this vile traffic they become odious and contemptible... But the most important of all lessons is the denunciation of ruin to every state that rejects the precepts of religion.[255]

Theism is the view that regards God as the intelligent Creator and Designer of a law-abiding universe. According to Michael V. Hernandez, '[t]he Founders were influenced by natural law thinking, principally the theories of John Locke, who grounded his *Second Treatise of Civil Government* in theism.'[256] Although not explicitly theistic, the U.S. Constitution reflected Christian values by ensuring liberty while prohibiting the establishment of religion and the imposition of religious tests for public office.[257] As Hernandez explains,

> The absence of overt theism in the Constitution did not reflect the intent to create a secular government. The Founders established a limited federal government in a Republic of preexisting state governments, not a

---

[255] Gouverneur Morris (1821), 'An Inaugural Discourse Delivered Before the New York Historical society by the Hon. Gouverneur Morris on September 4, 1816'. In *Collections of the New York Historical Society for the Year 1821* (New York/NY: E. Bliss & E. White), pp 32-4.

[256] Hernandez, above n.113, 909.

[257] Ibid.

comprehensive national governmental system. At the time the Constitution was drafted, state law and governmental systems were well established and explicitly theistic – some state laws even transgressed the proper boundaries of church and state by imposing Christian belief. The common law – which, as Blackstone's *Commentaries* made clear, was rooted in theism – served as the foundation for the states' laws.[258]

Although rationalism – particularly Deism – had some influence during the American revolutionary period, this historical fact is often misunderstood and its overall impact overstated.[259] The militant Deism of the likes of Thomas Paine never really threatened mainstream Protestantism in America's founding era.[260] Rather, vocal Deists such as Paine represented a tiny minority of individuals directly engaged in the political activities of the early Republic, the vast bulk of who were thoroughly orthodox in their Christian lives.[261]

Whereas most of these American leaders elaborated on certain Enlightenment ideals, such ideals were undeniably Enlightened Christian ideals of government and practical policy. The apparent conundrum, one might say, is found in the commonly held but ultimately misleading assumption that America's Enlightenment was somehow hostile to Christianity as it had been in the eighteenth century in France. This definitely was not the case in America since the tenor of the Enlightenment in those British colonies rarely rejected mainstream Christianity; quite to the contrary, even the Founders who were not so orthodox in their Christian faith (such as Benjamin Franklin and Thomas

---

[258] Ibid, p 910.
[259] Dreisbach and Hall, above n.23, p 6.
[260] Ibid, p 21.
[261] Ibid.

Jefferson) were fully able to appreciate Christianity as a positive force for society overall.[262]That the American Enlightenment was a profoundly Christian phenomenon is patently evident since it actually took place *within* the churches themselves.[263] As noted by Helena Rosenblatt,

> it should be stressed that these Enlightened Protestants started out convinced that their religion would be strengthened, not weakened, by its association with science and reason. Following the English example, Enlightened Protestants elsewhere came to believe that reason could and should be adopted as an indispensable aid to religion in its fight against 'enthusiasm' and superstition on the one hand, and deism on the other. To them, Locke's *Reasonableness of Christianity* (1695) provided invaluable tools, in fact often serving as a kind of unofficial lexicon of the Christian Enlightenment.[264]

The Anglo-American Enlightenment followed close on the heels of the Reformation. This was not intrinsically an anti-religious intellectual movement, but in essence a reasonable reaction against the established Catholic view of the world. Those Enlightenment thinkers could be found anywhere on the polarity between atheism materialism (Paine) and fairly

---

[262] 'In the middle of this period many elite Americans came to favour the beliefs and ideas associated with the European Enlightenment, while giving beliefs and ideas a cast favourable to Protestantism. Leaders of the Revolution and drafters of the Constitution – people of influence such as George Washington, John Adams, Thomas Jefferson, James Madison, and many more – while remaining responsible members of the Congressional churches in the north and the Anglican, later Episcopal, church in the south, breathed the spirit of this version of the Enlightenment'. – Marty, above n.168, pp 497-98.

[263] Helena Rosenblatt, 'The Christian Enlightenment', *in* Stewart J. Brown and Timothy Tackett (eds.), *Christianity: Enlightenment, Reawakening and Revolution 1660-1815* (Cambridge University Press, 2006) p 283.

[264] Ibid., p 285.

orthodox Christianity. In fact, writes David Daintree, 'the possibility of the elevation of humanity to a higher status (or its restoration to that status after the Fall) had always been part of Christian doctrine, so that Enlightenment thinking on that point could be squared with orthodox theology. The Christian doctrine of *theosis* or deification, little understood but perfectly orthodox, asserts that man's destiny is to be fully united with God. To this extent Enlightenment thinking might not be entirely inconsistent with Christianity'; quite to the contrary.[265]

Of the fifty-five delegates to the Constitutional Convention – 39 of whom signed the Constitution– not a single one of them can be fairly described as a non-Christian individual. Out of those 55, 31 were Episcopalians, 16 were Presbyterians, 8 were Congregationalists, 3 were Quakers, and 2 each were Methodists, Dutch Reform, Roman Catholics and Methodists. 2 of the signers of the constitution – Charles Pinckney of South Carolina and John Langdon of New Hampshire – were the founders of the American Biblical Society. Interestingly, James McHenry of Maryland was both the founder and inaugural President of the Baltimore Bible Society. Likewise, Rufus King of Massachusetts (another highly influential signer) established a Bible Society for the Episcopalian Church in his State.[266] When asked on the importance of obeying God's moral law, King stated that

> [t]he law established by the Creator extends over the whole globe, is everywhere and at all times binding upon mankind... This is the law of God by which he makes

---

[265] David Daintree, *Soul of the West: Christianity and The Great Tradition* (Ballarat/Vic: Connor Court Publishing, 2015), p 15.
[266] See Patrick Hynes, *In Defense of the Religious Right* (Thomas Nelson, 2006), pp. 52-3.

his way known to man and is paramount to all human control.[267]

In this sense, any claim that the U.S. Constitution was created in a complete divorce from religion positively cannot be substantiated. It is a profound misconception to maintain such an argument because it unreasonably denies the role Christian philosophy played in drafting all the leading documents in American constitutional history. This is no more evident than in the analysis of the American Bill of Rights; that is, the ten first amendments attached to the United States' Constitution. U.S. Supreme Court Chief Justice Earl Warren, who prior to serving the court was the only person ever elected three times as Governor of California, stated:

> I believe the entire Bill of Rights came into being because of the knowledge our Forefathers had of the Bible and their belief in it: freedom of belief, of expression, of assembly, of petition, the dignity of the individual, the sanctity of the home, equal justice under the law, and the reservation of powers to people.[268]

The tradition of the English *Magna Carta* profoundly influenced the American Bill of Rights. Part of Coke's *Second Institutes* (containing comments on Magna Carta) apparently first came to America on the Mayflower.[269] In substance, however, the document was closely modelled on the *Virginia Declaration of Rights* of 1776. Indeed, those constitutional rights to freedom of religion, freedom of the press and due process

---

[267] Charles R. King (ed) *The Life and Correspondence of Rufus King – Volume VI* (New York/NY: G.P. Putnam's Sons, 1900), p 276

[268] Former Chief Justice Earl Warren, Address to the Annual Prayer Breakfast, International Council of Christian Leadership, 1954. Quoted from DeMar, above n.40, p 1.

[269] Stoner, above n.88, p 13.

were all first seen in the *Virginia Declaration,* which set the template not only for the Declaration of Independence but also for the Bill of Rights of the U.S. Constitution. Section 16 of the *Virginia Declaration* proclaims:

> That religion, or the duty which we owe to our Creator, and the manner of discharging it, can be directed only by reason and conviction, not by force or violence; and therefore, all men are equally entitled to the free exercise of religion, according to the dictates of conscience; and that it is the mutual duty of all to practice Christian forbearance, love, and charity towards each other.

Considerable elements of Section 16 of the Virginian Declaration exhibit distinctly Christian influences. They had significant implications for the nature of the American Bill of Rights. In additional to the reference to 'our Creator' the Section commands that the free exercise of religion is to be granted in harmony with the principles of 'Christian forbearance, love and charity towards each other.' Expanding on this point, the drafters of the Bill of Rights can be seen, in reality, to promote and formally recognise these religious precepts through the provision. This is despite the fact that the section itself protects a right *not* to practice the Christian or any religious faith. Of course, the Bill of Rights attached to the U.S. Constitution omits the significant references to a Creator and Christianity, which are included in section 16. Even so, there can be no doubt that its drafters were men of faith who shared the same Christian values and convictions of the drafters of the *Virginia Declaration.* By relying on section 16 in the drafting of the First Amendment, they aimed to replicate the effect of that section, and are impliedly seen as invoking its expressly Christian justification.

In addition, the religious roots of the American Constitution can be traced back directly to the notion of covenant from the Jewish Torah. For the Jewish people, 'covenant was a mutually binding commitment by a group of freely consenting partners that set out a way of life rather than a matter of mere law and a way of life that was to lead to a just, free, peaceful and health commonwealth – in a word, to *shalon*, or human flourishing'.[270] Derived from the Hebrew Scriptures, and the American Puritan heritage which are inspired by those Scriptures, most early Americans believed that the 'constitution' is more than positive laws, however fundamental and clear these written annunciations might be. In its essence, at the root of the Protestant Reformation is the religious idea of covenant that has touched such countries as Switzerland, Scotland and Germany; and through the Puritans, 'it had shaped New England churches, then marriages, then townships, then colonies and finally the new nation itself'.[271] Indeed, as noted by the Christian philosopher, Os Guiness, 'the constitutional provisions for freedom in 1787 [were] sworn to with the same free consent and with the same binding commitment, they were designed to create "a more perfect union", a framework within which free citizens could live freely and peacefully – each "under his own vine", as George Washington expressed it in a direct echo of the Hebrew prophet Micah'.[272]

---

[270] Os Guinness, *A Free People's Suicide: Sustainable Freedom and the American Future* (Downers Grove/IL: IVP Books, 2012), p 51.
[271] Ibid.
[272] Ibid.

20

Biblical Foundations of American Federalism

Federalism also helps explain why religion is not explicitly mentioned in the US Constitution. Biblical principles indirectly inspired the American Founders to establish a federal model for their republican experiment. Federalism is primarily about the need of peoples and societies to unite for common purposes, yet to remain relatively separate so as to preserve their respective liberties and integrities. Accordingly, federal principles represent the delicate combination of self-government with the idea of shared rule, which seeks not just to protect national unity but also to maximize freedom and equality between the parties involved in the social compact. This so being, a true federation must derive from a pluralist concern for the fair distribution and share of governmental powers, as well as a strong emphasis on individual liberty and political participation. The matter is succinctly explained by James Madison in *Federalist No. 51*:

> In a single republic, all the power surrendered by the people is submitted to the administration of a single government; and the usurpations are guarded against by a division of the government into distinct and separate departments. In the compound republic of America, the

power surrendered by the people is first divided between two distinct governments, and then the portion allotted to each is subdivided among distinct and separate departments. Hence a double security arises to the rights of the people. The different governments will control each other, at the same time each will be controlled by itself.

The term 'federal' derives from the Latin word *foedus*, meaning covenant. Curiously, the Hebrew word *shalom* is both a word for peace and a cognate of the Hebrew *brit*, which also means covenant. Hence federalism can be seen as an outworking of the biblical idea of covenant, which essentially signals the partnership that it is both established and regulated by a social contract 'based on a mutual recognition of the integrity of each partner and the attempt to foster a special unity among them'.[273] As Daniel J. Elazar noted:

> The federal idea has its roots in the Bible. Indeed, the first usage of the term was for theological purposes, to define a partnership between man and God described in the Bible, which, in turn, gave form to the idea of a covenantal (of federal) relationship between individuals and families leading to the formation of a body politic and between bodies politic leading to the creation of compound polities. The political applications of the theological usage gave rise to the transformation of the term 'federal' into an explicitly political concept.[274]

The twelve tribes of Israel applied federal principles for the first time in history in the 13th century BC. Those ancient Hebrews sought to preserve their national unity by establishing a union of polities under the same federal framework. Although

---

[273] Daniel J. Elazar, *Exploring Federalism* (London/UK: The University of Alabama Press, 1987), p 5.
[274] Ibid.

the biblical account is obviously more religious than legal-philosophical-institutional, although the records of the Israelite federation in the Old Testament (particularly in the books of Pentateuch, Joshua, Judges, Samuel, and Ezekiel) provide a 'close insight to the operations of the Israelite tribal federation, describing its constitution, political institutions, and some of its central political problems, all within the framework of covenant theory.'[275] As Elazar pointed out:

> The Israelite example represented federalism in its most complete form: a people founded by covenant and a polity organized on federal principles. Although federal arrangements often are used to link peoples that do not have a covenantal bas and, conversely, some peoples founded by covenant or compact do no establish federal systems of government, federal systems are strongest when both are combined. That has continued to be the case throughout history.[276]

Inspired by the example of those ancient tribes of Israel, federalism was re-created in the 16th century as a form of federal theology by which, among other things, the Scottish Presbyterians, the English and American Puritans, and other Reformed groups were able to develop pluralist theories of government as well as pluralist principles of constitutional design.[277] During the first days of American colonial history, the history of the Israelite federation exercised a profound influence on the original settlers, particularly the Puritans. Above all, the biblical polity inspired the English Puritans who migrated to the New Continent – and later the Americans of the revolutionary

---

[275] Ibid, p 119.
[276] Ibid, p 120.
[277] Ibid, p 119.

period – to seek federal arrangements for their new political communities.[278] According to law professor Nicholas Aroney,

> [t]he early Puritans who settled in New England understood themselves as re-establishing society by covenant. They adopted covenants to organise their relationships within each local church and town, and federations of towns emerged in New England to form statewide governments. The covenants upon which these federations were based became the basis of the American state constitutions, which in turn provided the model for the Constitution of the United States. This tradition of written constitutionalism, especially as it developed in the United States, has become accepted throughout the world. While modern constitutionalism has drifted from these roots, we should not forget that the idea developed from essentially Christian origins.[279]

To conclude, it has been noticed that federalism as a system of civil or national government bears a close analogy to the Presbyterian and Reformed schemes of church government, just as hierarchical or Episcopal forms of church government correspond to monarchical models of civil government. As noted by Nicholas Aroney, 'the Presbyterian form of church government and federal systems of civil government endeavour to strike a careful balance between unity and centralised control on one hand, and diversity and independence on the other'.[280] These formal similarities between federalism and Presbyterianism are not merely a coincidence. As Aroney points out,

---

[278] Ibid, p 120.
[279] Nicholas Aroney, 'Society's Salt' (2008) 608 *Australian Presbyterian* 3, p 7.
[280] Nicholas Aroney, 'Australian Federalism', in Gregory I. Fraser (ed.), *Democracy Down Under: Understanding our Constitution* (Melbourne/Vic: Presbyterian Church of Victoria, 1997), p 10.

Within the same Reformation ear, a large number of important theologians, constitutional historians and publicists formulated widely influential theories of constitutional law which were covenantal and federal in orientation. Among them were a number of eminent Calvinists, including Theodore Beza, John Knox, Junius Brutus (pen-name, probably, of Philippe Duplessis-Mornay), George Buchanan, François Hotman, Samuel Rutherford and Johannes Althusius [...] Roman Catholics also joined in these arguments (eg, Juan de Mariana and Francisco Suarez) [...] Those who promulgated and acted on these theories deeply influenced the constitutional development of many nations, particularly those most touched by the Reformation, such as Switzerland, Germany, Holland, Scotland, England and, later, the United States. The European countries already had an orientation to federalism rooted in the medieval use of oaths and covenants as the binding forces of society. Reformed theology served to strengthen and extend this orientation. The theory of federalism took deep root in American soil, and the American model of federalism has since encircled the globe.[281]

---

[281] Ibid., p 15.

21

The Establishment Clause in the U.S. Constitution

There are countless examples of the American Founders pointing to their Christian faith as the cornerstone for their new country and its constitutional framework. It is against this background that the opening sentence of the First Amendment to the U.S. Constitution must be interpreted: 'Congress shall make no law respecting an establishment of religion or prohibiting the free exercise thereof'. Plainly and obviously, the First Amendment is basically a clause prohibiting the creation of a federal church, thus guaranteeing the free exercise of religion.

And yet, this Amendment has sometimes been identified as evidence that the Constitution should be regarded as entirely 'secular' in nature. But nothing could be further from the truth. The argument that the U.S. Constitution is entirely 'secular' finds itself in the absence from the document of the names of God and Christ. The argument appeals to a superficial anti-religious sentiment. First of all, we are dealing with a federal charter. Besides, the religious quality of a people is not measurable by phrases of law, but by the spirit and meaning of the law. Even if the American people should insert the divine name in their written constitution, this would not necessarily make theirs a more Christian nation. Nonetheless, all but two of the American state constitutions during the American Revolution explicitly contained the name of God. According to Sanford H. Cobb,

> If we would seek the religion of the American nation, we must look into their life, custom, and institutions. Looking on these things – the innumerable Christian temples and institutions of Christian charity, the days of annual thanksgiving, the prayers in legislative halls, the Bible in the courts, at the constant resort in legislation and judicature to religious and Christian principles, - we may safely declare that if the American people be not a Christian, there is noon upon the earth... This opinion has been shared by every statesman and every jurist who has discoursed on the subject. Marshall, Webster, Waite, and a host of others could all join in the language of Cooley, 'In a certain sense and for certain purpose, it is true that Christian is part of the law of the law'. It is impossible to fist the stigma on the American [Constitution].[282]

The idea of separation between church and state has its own historical roots in traditional Christian philosophy. In no way does the concept imply the exclusion of 'religious' perspectives from the political process. Actually, the concept itself can be traced not just to Scripture but also to the teachings of Jesus Christ himself. In Matthew 22:21 Christ is reported to have declared that citizens must 'render unto Caesar the things that are Caesar's, and to God the things that are God's.' Because some things are due to God alone, the state's claim upon human existence is limited,[283]which implies a separation between the

---

[282] Sanford H. Cobb, *The Rise of Religious Liberty in America: A History* (New York/NY: Macmillan Co., 1902), pp. 524-25.

[283] Harold O.J. Brown, 'The Christian American Position', *in* Gary Scott Smith (ed.), *God and Politics: Four Views on the Reformation of Civil Government* (Phillipsburg/NJ: Presbyterian and Reformed Publishing Co., 1989), p 146.

spiritual role of the church and the temporal role of the state. Such teaching is the root of religious freedom in America. As stated by Cobb in *The Rise of Religious Liberty in America* (1902):

> [T]his American principle, by which leaves the utmost liberty of religion and worship to the people, is in perfect harmony with the utterances of the great Founder of Christianity … To God alone is the man responsible for his religious views and practice. Under God only the man is ruler in his own mind and soul. This autonomy of souls even God Himself recognizes and respects, not compelling by external force, but appealing to reason, conscience and affection. Herein is the divine foundation for Religious Liberty. Its enactment by the American constitution is but a recognition of a law of God written in the nature of truth and of man. As such it is to be reckoned as their echo of the divine will, and fully as Christian an utterance as ever fell from the lips of government.[284]

Curiously, there was no significant distinction between sacred and secular in pre-Christian western societies. Ancient Greek and Roman societies, clearly, were not secular, but deeply religious. In Ancient Rome, the worship of the state in the person of the divine Emperor was the ideology that unified the Roman Empire. Roman law, and the resulting persecution of religious dissidents, corroborates that the only religions permitted in Rome were those licensed and approved by the state. As the law from the Twelve Tables (5th century BC) determined, 'Let no one have gods on his own, neither new ones nor strange ones, but only those instituted by the State.' Later, as David Daintree explains, 'it was typical of the ambitious politician to claim some kind of divine ancestry: Julius Caesar, for example, relied on a

---

[284]   Cobb, above n.279, pp.527-28.

claim to be descended from the goodness Venus, and following the overthrown of the Republic the practice arouse quite quickly of pretending (and no doubt in many cases actually believing) that deceased emperors had been deified and assumed into the pantheon of heaven'.[285]

The Greek polis and the Roman Empire were church-states. Statecraft was soul-craft for the ancient Greeks so that Socrates was executed by his fellow Athenian citizens precisely for being an Atheist; that is, for corrupting the youth by teaching them to doubt the gods of Athens. Others suffered similar fates, fates reserved to all those who defied the gods, which the definitions of law confirmed. Religious language and terminology were deeply infused in these definitions. For instance, note the celebrated Roman jurist and statesman Cicero's definition of law: 'To curtail this law is unholy, to amend it illicit, to repeal it impossible; ... and God, its designer, expounder and enactor, will be as it were the sole and universal ruler and governor of all things.'[286] Hence, in *The Ancient City* (1866) Fustel de Coulanges (1830–1889) commented that

> [i]t is a singular error to believe that in the ancient cities men enjoyed [religious] liberty. They had not even the idea of it. They did not believe that there could exist any right as against the city and its gods ... The ancients, particularly the Greeks, always exaggerated the importance, and above all, the rights of society [at the expense of the individual];this was largely due, doubtless, to the sacred and religious character which society was clothed in the beginning.[287]

---

[285]   Daintree, above n.265, p 8.
[286]   Marcus Tulius Cicero, *De Republica*, II. 22.23
[287]   Fustel de Colanges, *The Ancient City: A Study of the Religion, Laws and Institutions of Greece and Rome* (New York/NY: Dover Publications, 2006), p 223.

Whereas the concept of a 'secular state' was entirely unknown to the people of those ancient civilizations, there is substantial evidence tracing the concept of church-state separation to the Holy Bible. First of all, Christ did not equate the 'Kingdom of God' with any specific form of government, which makes it possible to establish a jurisdictional separation of church and state. Further, Christianity regards human redemption and virtue as a product of God's supernatural activity. Accordingly, 'the State became an administrator of justice under God's divine law, and men were to render to Caesar only those things that were Caesar's and to God what was God's.'[288] Such teachings were extremely revolutionary because, as above mentioned, the Greeks and Romans knew nothing about separating religion and state. Religion served for them mainly as an accessory of statecraft.

On the other hand, as Steven Alan Samson points out, 'the advent of Judaism and Christianity set new forces into motion that freed religious energies from a preoccupation with parochial loyalties.' According to Professor Samson, 'early Christians and Jews challenged the state cult of imperial Rome by refusing obeisance to Caesar as their lord or master. Both groups sought immunity from the religious laws and had to endure periods of official persecution while defending their distinct identity and way of life.'[289]That being so, Jesus's dictum that what belongs to God should not be given to Caesar come as a fundamental constraint to political tyranny. His words communicated the

---

[288] Gary Amos, 'The Philosophical and Biblical Perspectives that Shaped the Declaration of Independence', in H.W. House (ed.), *The Christian and American Law* (1998), p 56.

[289] Steven Alan Samson, 'Faustian Bargains: Entanglements Between Church and State in America', (2011) 2 *The Western Australian Jurist* 61, pp 88-9.

message that government had limited, not absolute power, so that 'Caesar could not demand worship that belonged to God.'[290] And since Rome rejected Christ's challenge to its claim to ultimate power, it retaliated by persecuting Christians.[291] As Dinesh D'Souza points out,

> [f]or the ancient Greeks and Romans, the gods a man should worship were the gods of the state. Each community had its own deities—it was a polytheistic age—and patriotism demanded that a good Athenian make sacrifices to the Athenian gods and a good Roman pay homage to the gods of Rome. The Christians, Celsus fumed, refused to worship the Roman gods. They did not acknowledge the Roman emperor as a god, even though Caesar had been elevated by the Roman Senate to divine status. Instead the Christians insisted on worshiping an alien god, putting their allegiance to him above their allegiance to the state.[292]

Although Christ was, perhaps, the first person ever to articulate the principle of separating religion and government, there was already a division of jurisdictional functions between civil and ecclesiastical powers in Ancient Israel. The Jewish king had the constitutional authority to enact civil laws, but he had no authority to legislate on religious issues. Not only was he explicitly prohibited from creating canon law, but the high priest himself was legally obliged to remind the monarch of his obligations under Mosaic Law. This contributed to a principle of just governance based on the constitutional division of government powers. 'By appointing Saul as king, the Israelites

---

[290] Vishal Mangalwadi, *The Book that Made Your World: How the Bible Created the Soul of Western Civilization* (Nashville/TN: Thomas Nelson, 2011), p 342.
[291] Ibid.
[292] Dinesh D'Souza, *What's so Great About Christianity* (New York/NY: Regnery, 2007), p 46.

established political authority independent of religious authority, by regulations codified by Moses.'[293] Dimont noted on this aspect of the legal code of the Old Testament:

> The Mosaic Code laid down the first principles for a separation of church and state, a concept not encountered again in world history until three thousand years later, during the Enlightenment in the eighteenth century of our era. In the Mosaic Code, the civil authority was independent of the priesthood. Though it is true that the priesthood had the right to settle cases not specifically covered by Mosaic law (Deuteronomy 17:8-12), that did not place it above the civil government. The priesthood was charged with the responsibility of keeping this government within the framework of the Mosaic law … Moses also laid the foundation for another separation, which has since become indispensable to any democracy. He created an independent judiciary.[294]

At least from the time of Moses down to the Babylonian captivity, the kings of Israel came from one particular tribe (Judah), whereas all the priests came from another tribe (Levi). This established a clear division of powers, although both political and ecclesiastical authorities were ultimately subject to the Mosaic Law. Of course, abuses occurred from the very beginning. The first appointed king was also the first to break jurisdictional boundaries, which had been created to legally protect the people of Israel from political tyranny. That being so, the Old Testament (1 Samuel 13) reports the episode when King Saul grew impatient waiting for the prophet Samuel, so he decided to offer religious sacrifices personally. The king was accused of overstepping his authority by attempting to fulfil

---

[293] Mangalwadi, above n.290, p 341.
[294] Max I. Dimont, *Jews, God and History* (2nd ed., Signet, 2004), pp 85-6.

a constitutional role exclusively designated for the religious leader. In addition, 1 Chronicles 26:20 explains that the Levites were the only ones in charge of the temple and the gifts devoted to God. By law the religious activities limited their sphere of activity and they were not directly responsible for the affairs of the state. This is not to say that there were no competing claims to the king's priesthood. In Psalm 110, which is a 'Coronation Psalm', the king is described 'as a priest forever according to the supreme order of Melchizedek.'

Be that as it may, relying on the teachings of Christ in the eleventh century the church started to demand further legal protections against the 'secular control'. Initiated by Pope Gregory VII in 1075, the Papal Revolution is the name provided to the movement that *gave birth to the modern Western concept of church-state separation*, which demanded the end of all government interference over the church's doctrinal and ecclesiastic affairs. According to Harold Berman, the Papal Revolution was responsible for laying down 'the foundation for the subsequent emergence of the modern secular state by withdrawing from emperors and kings the spiritual competence which they had previously exercised.'[295]

Although Christ was one of the first individuals in history to articulate the idea of separation between church and state, such division of powers between civil and ecclesiastical jurisdictions was already practiced in ancient Israel. Although the Hebrew kings had the authority to enact civil laws, they were prohibited to enact legislation on ecclesiastical matters. Those kings were prevented from creating or altering the canon law, and the high

---

[295] Harold J Berman, *Law and Revolution: The Formation of the Western Legal Tradition* (1983), p 115.

138

priest had the obligation to remind him of his political duties and limitations under the Mosaic Law. As such, institutional limitations had been developed between secular and spiritual powers, although the political and ecclesiastical authorities were ultimately subjected to the Mosaic Law.[296]

Inspired by these biblical lessons the American Founders envisaged federal separation between church and state at the federal level.[297] The Constitution, unlike any other early document in American legal history, indeed lacks overtly religious content. This constitutional protection of the church from government intervention was a truly revolutionary idea. As Samson points out, 'from the earliest days of the church, monarchs had often claimed authoritative powers in matters of church doctrine and government. The authority of the Roman emperor as the supreme pontiff over the state religion was maintained to some degree even as the empire became nominally Christian, though it was expressly repudiated by the Christian emperor, Gratian.'[298]

Of course, the first American colonists were Christian pilgrims who had been harshly persecuted by the English government on account of their religious convictions. In the hopes of freely practising their religious faith, they had fled England and persecution from the established Church. It is therefore unsurprising that the constitutional framers dreaded so much the influence of ecclesiastical powers in all political matters; a fear which their ancestors brought with them from

---

[296] However, abuses occurred since the first appointed king; he was the first to break these jurisdictional boundaries, which had been created to protect the people of Israel from political tyranny.

[297] Amos, above n.288, p 56.

[298] Samson, above n.289, p 69.

the parent country.[299] To ensure that the plight of their Christian ancestors would be more fully heard, the First Amendment was included and it reads: 'Congress shall make no law respecting an establishment of religion, or prohibiting the free exercise thereof...'

The First Amendment is the most well-known and debated amendment in the American Bill of Rights. It combines five civil liberties so as to condense the various proposals from the state ratifying conventions. These liberties are designed to limit the power of the central government. The first liberty protected by this amendment has received particular attention: 'Congress shall make no law respecting an establishment of religion, or prohibiting the free exercise thereof'. As can be seen, the provision limits only the federal legislature (i.e., Congress) so that the individual states were fully exempt, and they could, if their individual legislatures so desired, to create laws establishing any official church. As Robert A. Destro points out,

> The First Amendment was necessary to assure the critics of the new Constitution that Congress would not use its express or implied powers (such as commerce, taxation or spending) to make laws infringing State or individual prerogatives regarding religion. Necessarily included in this prohibition were federal attempts to establish a national religion or dis-establish the established religions of the States which had them, and to enact or enforce laws

---

[299]   Story, above n.161, p 259.

which sought to burden religious belief or practice.[300]

The main drafter of the First Amendment, James Madison, attempted to incorporate portions of the Bill of Rights into the state constitutions – for example prohibiting the establishment of State churches. The proposal was soundly rejected by Congress.[301] After that rejection Madison went on to propose that the word 'national' be inserted before 'religion'. Madison feared that one sect could obtain pre-eminence, or two combined together, to establish a national religion to which they would compel all others to conform. He thought that the word 'national', if introduced, 'would point the amendment directly to the object it was intended to prevent.'[302]

Since Virginia and North Carolina were the states that proposed the First Amendment guaranteeing religious freedom, their views deserve special consideration. The Virginia and North Carolina amendment proposals made the original meaning of the clause crystal clear: 'No particular religious sect or society ought to be favored or established by law, in preference to others.'[303] Their intention was simply that the federal legislature (i.e., Congress) should not be able to establish a 'Church of the United States' vis-à-vis the official

---

[300]   Robert A. Destro, 'The Structure of the Religious Liberty Guarantee' (1995) 11 *Journal of Law & Religion* 355, 371. Professor Destro also explains: 'Though there was some dispute among the framers, the States, and the antifederalists concerning the extent to which the enumerated powers of the federal government could be utilized to set national policy respecting establishments of religion and religious liberty, there was little dispute among them about the core of the matter: the powers granted the federal government did not include a specific supervisory jurisdiction over either religious matters generally, or the relationship of religion and religious institutions to the political communities of the Nation'. (at 359)

[301]   McClanahan, above n.153, p 182

[302]   Annals of Congress, 1ˢᵗ Session, 1ˢᵗ Congress: 758-59. Quoted in McClanahan, above n.153, p 182.

[303]   DAFC, III: 659; IV:244. Quoted in McClanahan, above n.154, p 182.

Church of England.

Of course, the proposal by no means implies that American public life should be entirely devoid of religious input.[304] To the contrary, 'there is a good reason to think that the principal purpose of the Establishment Clause, and maybe the sole one, was to protect the state religious establishments from disestablishment by the federal government.'[305]Like those who drafted the First Amendment, the drafters of the Fourteenth Amendment too were not advocating some radical new understanding of the doctrine of church and state. Rather, they aimed at prohibiting Congress to establish a federal church, lest their state churches be disestablished by act of Congress.[306] A further reason for the proposed clause was a desire to avert disunity among the several states because of the differences in theology and church structure.[307] As Russell Kirk noted,

> Had any one of these churches been established nationally by Congress, the rage of other denominations would have been irrepressible. The only security lay in forbidding altogether the designating of a national church. Surely the Union was shaky enough in 1790 without risking hostilities to the tune of fife and drum ecclesiastic. The clause was in no way a disavowal of the benefits of religious belief; it owed nothing to the atheistic preachments of

---

[304] In North Carolina, representative Henry Abbot equated 'religion' with any particular Christian denomination and North Carolina's governor Samuel Johnson contended that the 'religions' of the States included members of the Presbyterian, Baptist, and Episcopalian churches, as well as Quakers and other 'sects'. Many other members of the Convention used the word 'religion' in this particular way, since 'there was unanimity that morality and religion were bedrocks of a stable society'. – McClanahan, above n.153, p 182.
[305] Carter, above n.212, p 118.
[306] Kirk, above n.56, p.154.
[307] Ibid.

Diderot, D'Alembert, and other free Gallic spirits of the Enlightenment. It was out of expediency, not from anti-religious principle, that Congress accepted, and states ratified, the first clause of the First Amendment.[308]

Curiously, the disestablishment of the state churches that took place in the first half of the 19th century was intended to strengthen rather than impair the cooperation between church and state as institutions.[309]Numerous court rulings attest this, including the 1811 decision in *People v Ruggles* where the Supreme Court of New York noted that 'the people of this state, in common with the people of this country profess the general doctrines of Christianity as the rule of their faith and practice.'[310] Chief Justice Kent stated:

> Though the constitution has discarded religious establishments, it does not forbid judicial cognisance of those offences against religion and morality which have no reference to any such establishment, or to any particular form of government, but are punishable because they strike at the root of moral obligation and weaken the security of the social ties ... The legislative exposition of the constitution is conformable to this view of it.[311]

As can be seen, the American constitutional system is essentially Christian in its foundational character and assumptions. Justice William O. Douglas acknowledged this when he wrote that 'a 'religious' rite which violates standards of Christian ethics and morality is not in the true sense, in the constitutional sense, included within 'religion', the 'free

---

[308] Ibid, p 155.
[309] Samson, above n.289, p 66.
[310] *People v Ruggles* (8 Johns, R. 290 N.Y. (1811), at 296-297
[311] Ibid, 297.

exercise' of which is guaranteed by the Bill of Rights.'[312]From the bench, he reiterated the same assumption as recently as 1951. In *Zorach v Clauson*, speaking for a majority of the United States Supreme Court, Justice Douglas stated:

> We are a religious people whose institutions presuppose a Supreme Being ... To hold that government may not encourage religious instruction would be show a callous indifference to religious groups. That would be preferring those who believe in no religion over those who do believe ... We find no constitutional requirement which makes it necessary for government to be hostile to religion and to throw its weight against efforts to widen the effective scope of religious influence.[313]

The purpose of the First Amendment is therefore to prevent the establishment of a national 'Church of the United States'. In no way was the amendment intended to inhibit the power of the states to decide on religious matters as well as the constitutionally protected 'free exercise' of religion by the people. Once again, it is important to note that the drafters did not intend the establishment clause to be applied to the American states, but only to the federal government. The American states would have free rein on the issue, and most actually had either an established church or at least a strict religious test for office holders.[314] Thus, as Carter explains,

> [t]he legislative history leaves little doubt that the Clause, in all or its incarnations, was designed by the Founders to embody 'the jurisdictional concern of federalism' – to ensure that 'civil authority in religious affairs resided with

---

[312] William O. Douglas, *An Almanac of Liberty* (Garden City/NY: Doubleday and Co, 1954), 304.

[313] 343 U.S. 313-14 (1952).

[314] McClanahan, above n.153, p 184.

the states, not the national government'... Perhaps the best evidence of this original understanding is the fact that the established churches lingered on in the New England states long after the First Amendment was adopted.[315]

James Madison's original draft of what is now the Establishment Clause, introduced in the House of Representatives on 7 June 1789, read 'nor shall any national religion be established'. The final Senate version, prior to conference with the House, read 'Congress shall make no law establishing articles of faith or a mode of worship'.[316] As can be seen, the Founding Generation aimed to preserve the religious foundations of the American experiment by prohibiting only the federal government from establishing a National Church, such as the one still existing in England. Although the Constitution does not make an explicit tribute to God, in his *The American Commonwealth* James Bryce commented that 'Christianity [was] in fact understood to be, though not the legally [i.e., federally] established religion, yet the national [American] religion.'[317]

The Judeo-Christian deity was acknowledged in the state constitutions by the time of constitutional ratification, and the First Amendment certainly was not intended to change this situation. On the contrary, the establishment clause meant only to affect the federal parliament, 'placing no inhibition on the states, and leaving the whole subject to their uncontrolled discretion, though subject to the general guarantees against

---

[315] Carter, above n.212, p 298.
[316] All the drafts of the Clause appear as Appendix A in Edwin S Gaustad, Faith of Our Fathers: Religion and the New Nation (San Francisco: Harper & Row, 1987), pp.157-58.
[317] James Bryce, *The American Commonwealth* [1888], Vol.II, (Indianapolis/IN: Liberty Fund, 1995), p.1376.

oppression.'[318]For example, after declaring that 'all men are equally entitled to the free exercise of religion, according to the dictates of conscience', Article 16 of Virginia Declaration of Rights of 1776 communicated 'that it is the mutual duty of all to practice Christian forbearance, love, and charity towards each other.' As James Bryce explained:

> The early constitutions of several states recognized what was virtually a state church, requiring each locality to provide for and support the public worship of God. It was not till 1818 that Connecticut in adopting her new constitution placed all religious bodies on a level, and left the maintenance of churches to the voluntary action of the faithful. In Massachusetts a tax for the support of the Congregationalist churches was imposed on all citizens not belonging to some other incorporated religious body until 1811, and religious equality was first fully recognized by a constitutional amendment of 1833. In Virginia, North and South Carolina, and Maryland, Protestant Episcopacy was the established form of religion till the Revolution, when ... because the Anglican clergy were prone to Toryism (as attachment to the British connection was called) ... all religious distinctions were abolished and special ecclesiastical privileges withdrawn.[319]

The leaders of the American Revolution did not work to eliminate Christian influences on the nation. To the contrary, they made no attempt to change state constitutions that recognised the supremacy of God's law. After the American Revolution New Hampshire, Massachusetts, Connecticut, South Carolina and Maryland continued to have tax-supported

---

[318] Ibid, p 1370.
[319] Ibid, p 1372.

established churches.[320] Most of these state constitutions adopted a considerable degree of religious freedom, but few Americans in those days would conceive of a civil order which did not explicitly acknowledge the supremacy of God's law.[321] Even Pennsylvania, which had been one of the more liberal colonies in matters of religion, 'required that officeholders take an oath declaring the belief in the divine inspiration of the whole of the Bible'.[322] Below is what some of those state constitutions declared:

> Connecticut (until 1818): 'The People of this State ... by the Providence of God ... hath the sole and exclusive right of governing themselves as a free, sovereign and independent State ... and forasmuch as the free fruition of such liberties and privileges as humanity, civility, and Christianity call for us, is due to every man in his place and proportion ... hath ever been and will be the tranquillity and stability of Churches and Commonwealth; and the denial thereof, the disturbances, if not the ruin of both'
>
> Delaware (1831): Recognised 'the duty of all men frequently to assemble together for the public worship of the Author of the Universe'.
>
> Illinois (1870): 'We the people of the State of Illinois, grateful to Almighty God for the civil, political and religious liberty which he hath so long permitted us to enjoy and looking to Him for a blessing on our endeavors ... do ordain and establish this Constitution for the State of Illinois.'
>
> Maryland (until 1851): 'That, as it is the duty of every man to worship God in such a manner as he things most acceptable to him; all persons professing the Christian religion, are equally

---

[320] Forrest McDonald, *Novus Ordo Seclorum: The Intellectual Origins of the Constitution* (University Press of Kansas, 1985), p 43.
[321] Cobb, above n.282, pp.409-507.
[322] McDonald, above n.320, p 42.

entitled to protection in their religious liberty ... The legislature may, in their discretion, lay a general and equal tax, for the support of the Christian religion'.

North Carolina (1868): 'We, the people of the State of North Carolina, grateful to Almighty God the Sovereign Ruler of Nations, for the preservation of the American Union and the existence of our civil, political and religious liberties, and acknowledging our dependence on Him for the continuance of those blessings to us and our posterity, do, for the more certain securities therefore and for the better government of this State, ordain and establish this Constitution'. [323]

The language of these preambles is undeniably Christian in nature, affirming the duty of the state to support the predominant faith and providing the reasons for it. This continued to be so even after the U.S. Constitution was enacted, since the people of the new states which joined Federation, with the only exception of Oregon, recognised the supremacy of God and His Laws in the preambles of their respective constitutions. Oregon was the only exception but this does not mean its people were less Christian than those from the other states.[324]

Above all, the American Founders wished to allow the states decide on whether or not to establish religions. Certainly, they did not intend to proscribe state support for religion.[325] The

---

[323] For a list of state constitutions and their reference to the sovereignty of God, *see* Charles E. Rice, *The Supreme Court and Public Prayer: The Need for Restraint* (New York/NY: Fordham University Press, 1964), app. B.

[324] Lord Bryce wrote this about his travel to the state in 1881: 'In the chief city of Oregon I found ... that a person, and especially a woman of the upper class, who did not belong to some church and attend it pretty regularly, would be looked askance on. She need not actually lose case, but the fact would excite surprise and regret; and her disquieted friends would put some pressure upon her to enrol herself as a church member'. – Bryce, above n.317, p. 1387.

[325] Carter, above n.212, p 120.

states had reserved powers to themselves and the exclusive right to legislate on religious establishment. Some of these states had established churches and they continued to have so even many years after the enactment of the United States Constitution. According to Joseph Story, who served on the U.S. Supreme Court from 1811 to 1845, from its very foundation down to the American Revolution, in 1776, 'every former colony in the United States did openly, by the whole course of its laws and institutions, support and sustain in some form the Christian religion; and almost invariably gave a peculiar sanction to some of its fundamental doctrines.'[326] When other states joined the American federation after 1787, they too equally decided to acknowledge God in the preamble of their constitutions.[327]The acknowledgement of God in all state constitutions at the time of ratification indicates that Christian principles of law and justice actually inspired the drafters' protection of religious freedom.

The First Amendment in no way denies the importance of religion for society; for the principal purpose of the Establishment Clause in most of American history has been to protect religious freedom against the secular government.[328]In this context of religious pluralism and tolerance, the First Amendment was crafted to permit maximum freedom to the religion. This anti-establishment clause 'does not mean that people whose motivations are religious are banned from trying to influence government, nor that the government is banned

---

[326] Story, above n.161, p 629. Story also commented that, 'there would seem to be a peculiar property in viewing the Christian religion as the great basis on which [a republic] must rest for its support and permanence, if it be, what it has ever been deemed by its truest friends to be, the religion of liberty'

[327] Michael Novak and Ashley M. Novak, 'On the Square', *First Things*, February 5, 2006.

[328] Carter, above n. 212, p 108.

from listening to them.'[329] The amendment is therefore self-consciously theistic in its origin, a fact which the late Harvard professor of Political Theory, Samuel Huntington, succinctly explained:

> At the end of the eighteenth century, religious establishments existed throughout European countries and in several American states. State control of the church was a key element of state power, and the established church, in turn, provided legitimacy to the state. The framers of the American Constitution prohibited an establishment national church in order to limit the power of government and to protect and strengthen religion. The 'separation of church and state' is the corollary to the identity of religion and society.[330]

The original intention behind the First Amendment is not to establish freedom *from* religion, but rather to create freedom *for* religion. It explicitly prohibits a federal church to be established. Moreover, the idea of separating church and state was specifically designed to secure religious liberty, which Thomas Jefferson once called 'the most inalienable and sacred of all human rights.'[331] Thus, when Roger Williams wrote of the 'wall of separation between the garden of the Church and the wilderness of the world', he was merely expressing 'an ideal of toleration and religious plurality' that is reflected in 'the ability of the believer to worship without the interference of the state.'[332]

As noted by Chaput, 'Williams saw very clearly that

---

[329] Ibid, 106.

[330] Samuel Huntington, *Who are We?* (London: Free Press, 2005), p 85.

[331] Thomas Jefferson, 'Freedom of Religion at the University of Virginia', in Saul K. Padover (ed.), *The Complete Jefferson* (New York/NY: Duell, Sloan & Pierce, 1943), 958.

[332] Carter, above n.212, p 116.

Volume 2: The United States

agreement among the differing Christian sects of his day was unlikely. So Rhode Island formed a government committed to 'liberty of conscience'. Rather than settle religious disputes with civil law, Williams argued that the Christian duty was to learn to coexist.'[333]

The establishment clause should be interpreted against this historical background. It in no way implies that the United States should be governed by a 'secular government' devoid of any religious influence.[334]It was clear in those foundation days that the protection afforded by the First Amendment restrained only the legislative branch of federal government. In *The General Principles of Constitutional Law*, a work Thomas Cooley completed in March 1880 while Law Dean at Michigan University (Cooley later became Associate Justice of the Supreme Court of Michigan), he commented:

> By establishment of religion it was never intended… that the government should be prohibited from recognizing religion, or that religious worship should never be provided for in cases where a proper recognition of Divine Providence in the working of government might seem to require it, and where it might be done without drawing any invidious distinctions between different religious beliefs, organizations, or sects. The Christian religion was always recognized in the administration of the common law; and so far as that law continues to be the law of the land, the fundamental principles of that religion must continue to be recognized in the same cases and to the same extent as formerly.[335]

---

[333] Charles J. Chaput, *Render Unto Caesar: Serving the Nation by Living Our Catholic Beliefs in Political Life* (New York/NY: Image Books, 2008), p.81.
[334] Ibid.
[335] Thomas M. Cooley, *Principles of Constitutional Law*, Boston: Little Brown & Co., 1898, at 224.

151

The American Founders created a political system not derived from any particular statement of religious doctrine, although 'it was predominantly Christian in its legal assumptions, moral values, and religious sympathies.'[336] The framers of the U.S. Constitution did not wish to suppress religious argument from political debates. On the contrary, the vast majority of them believed that the connection between politics and faith was a particularly important thing for both public morality and good governance. They supported the right of every citizen to promote his or her own religious values in the political realm. That being so, the first federal legislature which enacted the First Amendment took a special care to re-enact the Northwest Ordinance of 1787, permitting the federal government to promote religious education in all public schools in the Northwest Territory: 'Religion, morality and knowledge, being necessary to good government and the happiness of mankind ... shall be forever encouraged.'[337]

Since those first federal legislators saw religion and education as going hand-in-hand, on 24 September 1787, the day after the first U.S. House of Representatives enacted the First Amendment, another resolution was proclaimed which called the new nation for a National Day of Prayer and Thanksgiving. Hence the traditional day of prayer and thanksgiving was inaugurated; a public holiday that the Americans celebrate up to this very day. It is worth reflecting on the symbolism of that gesture as well as on the words of that resolution, since this is the way in which the Founders expected the First Amendment to be applied: 'We acknowledge with grateful hearts the many

---

[336] Samson, above n 289, pp 61 and 66.
[337] See: John Baker, 'Establishment of Religion', in Edwin Mase III et al. (ed.), *The Heritage Guide to the Constitution* (Washington/DC: Regnery, 2005), p 302.

signal favors of Almighty God, especially by affording them an opportunity peacefully to establish a constitutional government for their safety and happiness.'[338] The argument goes in line with the personal thoughts of George Washington who, being the first President of the United States, officially declared

> [i]t is the duty of all nations to acknowledge the providence of Almighty God, to obey His will, to be grateful for His mercy, to implore His protection and favour ... That great and glorious Being who is the beneficent author of all the good that was, that is, or that ever will be, that we may then unite in rendering unto Him our sincere and humble thanks for His kind care and protection of the people.[339]

It is against this background that the First Amendment should be interpreted. Far from conceiving a 'godless' society, the drafters of that Amendment regarded the promotion of religion as fundamental for the preservation of the new republican government, since it was the same congress that passed the Amendment that also considered it suitable to declare public days of prayer and to appoint chaplains to the new federal legislature. Unfortunately, however, in more recent years the U.S. Supreme Court has misinterpreted the First Amendment by incorrectly placing the establishment and free-exercise clauses in mutual tension.[340] Such extravagant view is

---

[338] *Documentary History of the First Federal Congress*, Baltimore, 1977, pp 228-232, quoted in Johnson, above n.15, p 209.

[339] Thanksgiving Proclamation, 3 October 1789, quoted in Johnson, above n.15, p 209.

[340] There are a number of excellent books that examine the interaction between the state and religion in the United States. Examples include Cole Durham and Brett Scharffs' *Law and Religion: National, International, and Comparative Perspectives* (Aspen/Wolters Kluwer, 2010); Kent Greenawalt's *Religion and the Constitution – Volume 2: Establishment and Fairness* (Princeton and Oxford: Princeton University Press, 2008); and Michael W McConnell, John H Garvey and Thomas C Berg's *Religion and the Constitution* (New York: Aspen & Business, 2002)

not what the constitutional framers had in mind, although it has been achieved 'by relatively recent judicial activism which may be reversed as new judges are appointed.'[341] As noted by law professor John Baker:

> In recent years the Supreme Court has placed the Establishment and the Free Exercise of Religion Clauses in mutual tension, but it was not so for the Framers. None of the Framers believed that a government connection to religion was an evil in itself. Rather, many (though not all) opposed an established church because they believed that it was a threat to the free exercise of religion. Their primary goal was to protect free exercise [of religion]. Nor did most of the Founding generation believe that government ought to be 'untainted' by religion, or ought not to take an interest in furthering the people's connection to religion. The Northwest Ordinance (1787), which the First Congress re-enacted, stated: 'Religion, morality, and knowledge, being necessary to good government and the happiness of mankind, schools and the means of education shall forever be encouraged.[342]

Above all, writes by Paul Johnson, in a *A History of the American People*:

> The First Amendment... has been widely, almost wilfully, misunderstood in recent years, and interpreted as meaning that the federal government is forbidden by the Constitution to countenance or subsidize even indirectly the practice of religion. That would have astonished and angered the Founding Fathers. What the guarantee means is that Congress may not set up a state religion on the lines of the Church of England, 'as by law established'. It

[341] David Flint, 'Church and State', ACM, 03 April 2007.
[342] John Baker, 'Establishment of Religion', in Edwin Meese III et al (ed.), The Heritage Guide to the Constitution (Washington/DC: Regnery Publishing Co., 2005), p.302.

was an anti-establishment clause. The second half of the guarantee means that Congress may not interfere with the practice of any religion, and it could be argued that recent interpretations of the First Amendment run directly contrary to the plain and obvious meaning of this guarantee, and that for a court to forbid people to hold prayers in public school is a flagrant breach of the Constitution. In effect, the First Amendment forbade Congress to favor one church, or religious sect, over another. It certainly did not inhibit Congress from identifying itself with the religious impulse as such or from authorizing religious practices where all could agree on their desirability.[343]

21.1. The Doctrine of Incorporation

Freedom of religion is the first freedom in the American Bill of Rights, but it was for generations a freedom against Congress only. At the time the U.S. Constitution was adopted, several states had official churches; and Congress wrote the amendment that was the first to be ratified by the states so as to permit these establishments to continue while forbidding Congress to establish a national church: 'Congress shall make no law respecting an establishment of religion, or prohibiting the free exercise thereof''.

In 1833 Justice John Marshall for the U.S. Supreme Court laid down the rule that the first ten 'amendments contain no expression indicating an intention to apply them to the states. This Court cannot so apply them.'[344] As can be seen, the main goal of the free exercise clause of the First Amendment is to keep the federal government, in particular its legislative branch,

---

[343] Johnson, above n.15, p 209.
[344] *Barron v. Baltimore*, 7 Peters 243 (1833). This case was not concerned with religion.

from interfering in the religious matters (and laws) of the American states. In 1868, however, the Fourteenth Amendment was ratified by the states. It is one of the longest amendments, but only one sentence is important for us:

> No state shall make or enforce any law which shall abridge the privileges or immunities of citizens of the United States, nor shall any state deprive any person of life, liberty, or property without due process of law, nor deny to any person within its jurisdiction the equal protection of the laws.[345]

As a result, the Supreme Court has extended the reach of the First Amendment to the American states through the use of the Incorporation Doctrine within the Fourteenth Amendment. Accordingly, in *Cantwell v. Connecticut* (1940)[346]the court took the Free Exercise Clause ('Congress shall make no law ... prohibiting the exercise of religion') to mean that by arresting a religious person the state of Connecticut had violated his First Amendment rights. The case involved the prosecution of a Jehovah's Witness, Newton Cantwell, for disturbing the peace by going door-to-door on behalf of his religion and playing an anti-Catholic record in a Catholic neighbourhood.[347]

In the aftermath of *Cantwell* the citizens acquired by means of 'incorporation' identical First Amendment rights

---

[345] Dayton D. McKean, 'State, Church, and Lobby', in James Ward Smith and A. Leland Jamison (eds), *Religious Perspectives in American Culture* Princeton/NJ: Princeton University Press, 1961), p 128.

[346] 310 U.S. 296 (1940) (striking down the convictions of Jehovah's Witnesses for violating a statute against the solicitation of funds for religious, charitable, or philanthropic purposes without prior approval of public officials). *But see Barron v. Mayor and City Council of Baltimore*, 32 U.S. 243 (1833) (holding that the Bill of Rights was inapplicable to the states since its history demonstrated that it was limited to the Federal government).

[347] Kevin R.C. Gutzman, *The Politically Incorrect Guide to the Constitution* (Washington/DC: Regnery Publishing, 2007), p 175.

regardless of whether they challenge the actions of the federal or state governments over the establishment or free exercise of religion.[348] Unrelated to the Constitution's language and history, the 'incorporation doctrine' has been used (and abused) by the federal courts to invalidate a myriad of instances of state social policy.[349] Incorporation has become the court's main subterfuge to ignore the plain fact that the Bill of Rights was ratified to limit the powers of the federal government.

According to advocates of the incorporation doctrine, however, Barron was good law only until 1868, when the Fourteenth Amendment was ratified. After the Fourteenth Amendment was enacted no American state can deprive a person of life, liberty or property without due process, arguably making the First Amendment enforceable by federal courts against the states.[350] This allowed the federal courts to apply the Fourteenth Amendment's due process clause to completely redefine church-state relations, thus bringing more of it under the court's own purview and that of the federal government.[351] And yet, still twenty years after the Fourteenth Amendment was enacted, all the six Southern states of the United States *excluded* from public office anyone who denied the existence of God. Pennsylvania and Arkansas went even further by making atheists incompetent as both jurors and witnesses to court cases. Writing contemporaneously on such issues, Lord Bryce explained:

> [T]he Americans are more practically easygoing than

---

[348] Although issues associated with the practice of religion are more likely to be covered by the Free Exercise Clause, such disputes are often referred to as Establishment Clause disputes.
[349] Gutzman, above n.347, p 172.
[350] Ibid, p 172.
[351] Ibid, p 175.

pedantically exact, the national government and the state governments do give to Christianity a species of recognition inconsistent with the view that civil government should be absolutely neutral in religious matters. [352]

Since the 1990s the Supreme Court decisions are often based on a 'neutrality principle', which assumes that 'only a state that views itself as a 'homestead for all citizens' without committing itself to... contents of [any] one religion or creed can ensure freedom for each individual citizen'.[353] These decisions are based on the application of a principle which 'inherently trivializes ... religion because it largely results in the removal of religious influences from American society'. Because its application requires the State to be free from religion (rather than religion to be free from government interference),[354] such a principle inevitably degrades religion even 'to the point of making it irrelevant'. As noted by Gabriël A. Moens:

> Although, arguably, the use of the neutrality principle was developed to safeguard religious liberty, it has instead resulted in a failure to protect religion. Therefore, the Supreme Court's jurisprudence has the unfortunate

---

[352] Bryce, above n.317, p 1375.
[353] Gabriël A. Moens, 'The Menace of Neutrality in Religion' (2004) 12 *Brigham Young University* 535, p 567. According to Professor Moens, '[t]he Supreme Court first announced the neutrality principle as such in *Rosenberber v. Rector & Visitors of the University of Virginia* [515 U.S. 819 (1995)]. In *Rosenberger*, the University of Virginia (University), a state instrumentality, authorized payments from its Student Activities Fund (SAF) to outside contractors to cover the printing costs of a variety of publications issues by student groups. However, the University withheld authorization for payments to a printer for Rosenberger, of Wide Awake Productions (WAP), on the ground that, contrary to SAF guidelines, the journal had religious editorial content. In a 5-4 decision, the Supreme Court held that this action represented view point discrimination because it required University officials to scan and interpret student publications to ascertain their underlying philosophic assumption respecting religious theory and belief.' – p 544.
[354] Ibid., p 567.

consequence of facilitating the emergence of a culture of disbelief, making it difficult, if not impossible, to talk about religion in the legal context, or to talk about religion at all. Use of the neutrality principle has treated religion and religious belief as less important facets of the human personality. The recent focus on neutrality in issues between church and state, and likewise the trivialization of citizens' religious beliefs, moves counter to the philosophies upon which the United States was founded. In attempting to protect government from religion, only the latter has remained powerful in any degree.[355]

By contrast, early members of the American judiciary often cited Chief Justice Sir Matthew Hale's maxim that 'Christianity is parcel of the laws of England',[356] both in their written opinions and their scholarly commentaries. In his treatise on constitutional limitations, Chief Justice Cooley of the Supreme Court of Michigan stated: 'The Christian religion was always recognized in the administration of the common law; and so far as that law continues to be the law of the land, the fundamental principles of that religion must continue to be recognized in the same cases and to the same extent as formerly.'[357]Until the first decades of the twentieth century both the federal and state courts regarded that the administration of the law required acknowledging Christianity as being the nation's prevailing religion. This ample evidence led Joseph Story of the U.S. Supreme Court, who had previously taught constitutional law at Harvard University, to affirm '[t]hat there never has been a period, in which the Common Law did not recognise

---

[355] Ibid.,pp 567-68.
[356] *Taylor's Case*, 1 Vent. 293, 86 Eng. Rep. 189 (K.B. 1676).
[357] Thomas M. Cooley, *A Treatise on the Constitutional Limitations Which Rest Upon the Legislative Power of the States of the American Union – Volume 2* (8th ed., Boston/MA: Little, Brown, and Co., 1958), p 91.

Christianity as lying at its foundations.'[358]

By the time of constitutional ratification and ensuing inclusion of the First Amendment, Story reminded us that 'the universal sentiment in America was that Christianity ought to receive encouragement from the state so far as was not incompatible with the private rights of conscience and the freedom of religious worship.'[359] Justice Story then explains that 'the real object' of the First Amendment is 'not to prostrate Christianity but to exclude all rivalry among Christian sects, and to prevent any national ecclesiastical establishment which should give to a hierarchy the exclusive patronage of the national government.'[360] In other words, the intent behind the amendment was to advance religious freedom by excluding all the rivalry among the Christian groups so as to prevent the establishment of a national state-controlled Church.[361]

Until the early 20th century legal writers often claimed that 'Christianity is a fundamental part and parcel of the common law.' American judges and lawyers often repeated the maxim, citing numerous cases as support.[362] In *People v Ruggles* (1811), Chief Justice James Kent of the Supreme Court of New York

---

[358] Joseph Story, *Discourse Pronounced Upon the Inauguration of the Author, as Dane Professor of Law in Harvard University*, August 25th, 1829, in Herbert W. Titus, 'God's Revelation: Foundation for the Common Law', (1994) 4 *Regent University Law Review* 1, 3.

[359] Story, above n.161, p 630.

[360] Ibid., pp 631-2

[361] Ibid.

[362] Nathan Dane, *A General Bridgenement and Digest of American Law – Vol.6* (Boston: Cummings, Hilliard & Co., 1823), pp 667, 675; Joseph Story, 'Christianity a Part of the Common Law' (1833) 9 *The American Jurist*, 346; Theodore Sedgwick, *A Treatise on the Rules which Govern the Interpretation and Application of Statutory and Constitutional Law* (New York: J.S. Voorhies, 1857), 17; Christopher G. Tiedeman, *A Treatise on the Limitations of Police Power in the United States* (St Louis: F.H. Thomas Law Book Co., 1886), p 167.

declared that 'Christianity is a parcel of the law' in England. The only question remaining was whether the doctrine was part of the law of New York as well. According to Kent, no reason suggested the contrary because, in the state of New York as in England, 'Christianity, in its enlarged sense, as a revealed and taught in the Bible, is not unknown to our law.'[363] In Kent's view, '[Americans] are a Christian people, and the morality of the country is deeply engrafted upon Christianity.' However, merely questioning the truth of the Christian doctrine, in a reasonable manner, did not violate the common law. It was a crime only to revile the Christian religion 'with malicious and blasphemous content', although any similar attack on a religion such as Islam, or any other religion, was perfectly legal.[364] The state was not, in Justice Kent's opinion,

> bound, by any expressions in the constitution, as some have strangely supposed, either not to punish at all, or to punish indiscriminately the like attacks upon the religion of Mahomet [...]; and for this plain reason, that ... we are a Christian people, and the morality of the country is deeply engrafted upon Christianity, and no upon the doctrines or worship of [...] impostors.[365]

The American courts throughout the nineteenth century often repeated the maxim that 'Christianity is part and parcel of the common law' (or some variant thereof). Later commentators referred to this as a matter 'decided over and over again'; one in which 'these writers have reiterated and courts have affirmed.'[366] Christianity was then judicially recognised as part of the

---

[363] *People v Ruggles,* 8 Johns. 290, 293 (N.Y. 1811), 297.
[364] Ruggles, 8 Johns, p 295.
[365] Ibid.
[366] Stuart Banner, 'When Christianity Was Part of the Common Law' (1998) 16 *Law & History Review* 27, p 27.

common law by the Supreme Courts in Pennsylvania, Delaware, South Carolina, Arkansas, Tennessee, North Carolina, and Alabama.[367] The Delaware Supreme Court declared Christianity to be 'the foundation' of both the state's constitution and 'many of the principles and usages, constantly acknowledged and enforced, in the Courts of justice.' Similarly, the Georgia Supreme Court stated that the Bible is 'the foundation of the Common Law.'[368] And Daniel Webster, a lawyer and leading American senator, arguing before the Pennsylvania Supreme Court commented that 'there is nothing that we look for with more certainty than this general principle that Christianity is part of the law of the land.'[369] Webster justified his opinion as follows:

> *Everything supports it.* The massive cathedral of the Catholic; the Episcopalian church, with its lofty spire pointing heavenward; the plain temple of the Quaker; the log church of the hardy pioneer of the wilderness; the mementoes and memorials around and about us; the consecrated graveyards, their tombstones and epitaphs, their silent vaults, their mouldering contents; all attest it. *The dead prove it as well as the living.* The generation that are gone before speak to it, and pronounce if from the tomb. We feel it. All, all, proclaim that Christianity, general, tolerant Christianity, Christianity independent of sects and parties, that Christianity to which the sword and the fagot are unknown … is the law of the land.[370]

---

[367] Updegraph v Commonwealth, 11 Serg. &Rawle 394 (Pa. 1824); State v Chandler 2 Del. (2 Harr.) 553 (Del.1873); City Council of Charleston v Benjamim, 33 S.C.L. (2 Strob.)

[368] Ibid, p 50.

[369] Daniel Webster, 'The Writings and Speeches of Daniel Webster', vol.11 (1903), p 176.

[370] Ibid.

By the end of the nineteenth century any American writer could confidently assert that 'the preposition, that Christianity is part of the common law, is supported by the very highest judicial authority both in England and in this country.'[371] The maxim even received the formal endorsement from the Supreme Court of the United States, which affirmed in 1844 that 'the Christian religion is part of the common law.'[372]Five decades later, in *Church of Holy Trinity v the United States* (1892), the Supreme Court would decide that the administration of the American common law required acknowledging Christianity as the nation's prevailing religion. After a careful consideration of hundreds of court cases, state constitutions and other historical documents, the court unanimously held that 'these and many other which might be noticed add a volume of unofficial declarations to the mass of organic utterances that this is a Christian nation.'[373]Delivered by Justice Josiah Brewer, the court came to the following conclusion:

> Our laws and our institutions must necessarily be based upon and embody the teachings of the Redeemer of mankind. It is impossible that it should be otherwise; and in this sense and to this extent our civilization and our institutions are emphatically Christian... This is a religious people. This is historically true. From the discovery of this continent to the present hour, there is a single voice making this affirmation ... We find everywhere a clear recognition of the same truth ... These, and many other matters which might be noticed, add a volume of unofficial declarations to the mass of organic utterances that this is a Christian

---

[371] P. Emory Aldrich, 'The Christian Religion and the Common Law', (1889) 6 *American Antiquarian Society Proceedings* 18, pp 33-34.
[372] *Vidal v Philadelphia*, 43 U.S. 127, 198.
[373] *Church of the Holy Trinity v The United States* (1892) 143 US 457.

nation.[374]

Even to this very day the United States still retains a host of reminders of its rich religious history.[375] For example, for many years U.S. Congress allowed Christian Sunday worship services to be conducted in the Capitol itself. These services were regularly held when Thomas Jefferson was President. Not only he attended the religious services but the Marine band played in them. What is more, Christian worship was often held in the Supreme Court building.[376] As noted by the Library of Congress: 'Throughout his administration Jefferson permitted church services in executive branch buildings. The Gospel was also preached in the Supreme Court chambers.'[377]

And even to this very day Congress continues to employ chaplains for both Houses[378] and Senate,[379] who open sessions of Congress with prayer. The Supreme Court opens with the invocation of God.[380] Courtroom oaths end with the words, 'So help me God',[381] as do statutory oaths for federal judges,[382]

---

[374] Ibid.

[375] 'There is an unbroken history of official acknowledgment by all three branches of government of the role of religion in American life from at least 1789.' Lynch v. Donnelly, 465 U.S. 668, 674 (1984). Chief Justice Burger went on to discuss many of the examples we discuss here, *id.*at 675–78.

[376] Wayne Grudem, *Voting as a Christian: The Social Issues* (Grand Rapids/MI: Zondervan, 2012), at 190.

[377] 'The State Becomes the Church: Jefferson and Madison', Part VI: Religion and the Federal Government.

[378] 2 U.S.C.S. § 84-2 (2009). See the history of congressional chaplains in Marsh v. Chambers, 463 U.S. 783 (1983) (finding the employment of chaplains by a state legislature constitutional).

[379] 2 U.S.C.S. § 61d (2009).

[380] 'God save the United States and this honourable court.' *See* Zorach v. Clauson, 343 U.S. 306, 313 (1952) (citing this practice in support of the conclusion, 'We are a religious people whose institutions presuppose a Supreme Being.'). Judicial Centre, Benchbook for U.S. District Court Judges

[381] *See* Zorach v. Clauson, 343 U.S. 306, 313 (1952); Judicial Centre, Benchbook for U.S. District Court Judges(4th ed. 2000) 221–27.

[382] 28 U.S.C.S. § 453 (2009) (judges and magistrates).

court clerks,[383] and other elected officials.[384] The national motto proclaims, 'In God we trust'[385] and is displayed on all U.S. coinage.[386] The national Pledge of Allegiance includes the words, 'one nation, under God.'[387] The national anthem, adopted by statute, includes an entire verse about divine preservation of the nation.[388] By statute, the first Thursday in May is declared a national day of prayer.[389] Gary DeMar completes the list of official references to the Christian religion:

> The Ten Commandments hang over the head of the Chief Justice of the Supreme Court ... The crier who opens each session of the Supreme Court closes with the words, 'God save the United States and the Honorable Court'... In the Capitol Building a room was set aside ... to be used exclusively for the private prayer and meditation of members of Congress. In this specifically designated room there is a stained-glass window showing George Washington kneeling in prayer. Behind Washington a prayer is etched; 'Preserve me, O God, for in Thee do I put my trust' (Ps. 16:1). The two lower corners of the window

---

[383] 28 U.S.C.S. § 951 (2009).
[384] 5 U.S.C.S. § 3331 (2009) (federal elected or appointed officials other than the president).
[385] 36 U.S.C. S. § 302 (2009). Upheld against constitutional challenges in Aronow v. United States, 432 F.2d 242 (9th Cir. 1970), Gaylor v United States, 74 F3d 214 (D. Colo. 1996), and Newdow v. Cong. of the United States, 435 F. Supp. 2d 1066 (E.D. Cal. 2006).
[386] 31 U.S.C.S. § 5112 (d) (1) (2009), 31 U.S.C. S. § 5114 (b) (2009).
[387] 4 U.S.C. S. § 4 (2009). The constitutionality of this statement has been litigated in the circuit courts, with a split of opinion. Sherman v. Community Consolidated School Dist. 21, 980 F.2d 437 (7th Cir. 1992) upheld the Pledge's constitutionality; Newdow v. U.S. Congress, 328 F.3d 466 (9th Cir. 2002) struck it down. *Newdow* was reversed on appeal to the Supreme Court on standing issues. Elk Grove Unified School District v. Newdow, 542 US 1, 52–53 (2003). The Supreme Court has not resolved the substantive question.
[388] 36 U.S.C.S. § 301 (2009). *See* Santa Fe Indep. Sch. Dist. v. Doe, 530 U.S. 290, 322–23 (2000) (Rehnquist, C.J., dissenting) (suggesting that the national anthem's final verse is as religious as the prayer at issue in the case).
[389] 36 U.S.C.S. § 119 (2009).

165

show the Holy Scriptures and an open book and a candle, signifying the light from God's law: 'Thy Word is a lamp unto my feet and a light unto my path (P.s119:105)…In the House and Senate chambers appear the words, 'In God We Trust'. In the Rotunda is the figure of the crucified Christ. On the walls of the Capital dome, these words appear: 'The New Testament according to the Lord and Savior Jesus Christ'. On the Great Seal of the United States is inscribed the phrase *Annuit Coeptis*, 'God has smiled on our undertaking'. Under the Seal is the phrase from Lincoln's Gettysburg address: 'This nation under God'. President Eliot of Harvard chose Micah 6:8 for the walls of the nation's library. He hath showed thee, O man, what is good; and what doth God require of thee, but to do justly, and to lover mercy, and to walk humbly with thy God'. Engraved on the metal cap on the top of the Washington Monument are the words: 'Praise be to God'. Lining the walls of the monument's stairwell are numerous Bible verses: 'Search the Scriptures', 'Holiness to the Lord', and 'Train up a child in the way he should go, and when he is old he will not depart from it'. At the opposite end of the Lincoln Memorial, words and phrases of Lincoln's Second Inaugural Address allude to 'God', the 'Bible', 'Providence', the 'Almighty', and 'divine attributes'.[390]

Traditionally, U.S. presidents add the words, 'So help me God', to their oath of office, and ministers begin the inauguration ceremonies with prayer.[391] Furthermore, most presidents have issued proclamations with religious references.[392] 'The president is authorised to proclaim at least two Nation Day of Prayer each

[390] Gary DeMar, 'The Theonomic Response to National Confessionalism', *in* Gary Scott Smith (ed.), *God and Politics: Four Views on the Reformation of Civil Government* (Phillipsburg/NJ: Presbyterian and Reformed Publishing Co., 1989), p 202.
[391] Ibid. 2106–2109.
[392] *Lynch v. Donnelly*, 465 U.S. 668, 675–76 (1984).

year. Public law 82-324 requires the U.S. President to proclaim a National Day of Prayer on a day other than a Sunday. Under Public Law 77-379 the President proclaims the fourth Thursday of November each year as National day of Thanksgiving. The words 'under God' were inserted into the Pledge of Allegiance by Congress in 1954'.[393]

One might even consider a mistake to believe that such proclamations make America a Christian nation or that an absence of them would make it a non-Christian nation.[394]And yet, the fact is that, from George Washington to Donald Trump, U.S. presidents have always been sworn into office with their hands on an open Bible. Have their actions reflected the understanding that the U.S. has a secular government? For example, President Ronald Reagan declared 1983 to be 'The Year of the Bible' after the Senate and House of Representatives authorised and requested him to do so. This Joint Resolution stated:

> The Bible, the Word of God, has made a unique contribution in shaping the United States as distinctive blessed nation … deeply held religions convictions springing from the Holy Scriptures led to the early settlement of our Nation … Biblical teachings inspired concepts of civil government that are contained in our Declaration of Independence and the Constitution of the United States … the history of our nation clearly illustrates the value of voluntarily applying the teachings of the Scriptures in the lives of individuals, families and societies.[395]

Numerous official pronouncements speak clearly and

---

[393] DeMar, above n.390, p 202.
[394] Ibid. p 201.
[395] Public Law 97-280, 96 Stat. 1211, approved October 4, 1982. Quoted from DeMar, above n.387, p 201.

loudly about the religious character of the United States, which is quintessentially a Christian nation founded upon the principles of Christianity. Of course, the idea of America having been founded as a Christian nation and still being a Christian nation does not mean that every citizen is expected to be a Christian or to go to church. Rather, this is simply to say that Christianity was, and it still is, the religion of the majority or, more accurately, the stated religion of the majority. 'Being a Christian nation has to do with an ideal, with morality and what its inhabitants base it on'.[396]

This undeniable Christian heritage is displayed on nearly every page of America's constitutional history. As federal judge Frank McGarr observed in 1984: 'The truth is that America's origins are Christian with the result that our fondest traditions as Christian, and that our founding fathers intended and achieved full religious freedom for all within the context of a Christian nation in the First Amendment as it was adopted, rather than as we [judges] have rewritten it.[397] Judge McGarr was simply expressing the view that his country began its existence as a proudly Christian nation, despite such an obvious observation being presently ignored or neglected by activist judges who prefer to base their decisions on a particular (mis)reading of the nation's history and its constitution.

In more recent decades the American courts have deliberately attempted to place the establishment clause and promotion of religion in mutual tension. In *Everson v Board of Education* (1947) Justice Hugo Black interpreted the First

---

[396] Janet Pope, *It's Though to Breath With Your Head in the Sand: Facing the Moral Decline of Our Culture* (Maitland/FL: Xulon Press, 2005)
[397] Cited in DeMar, above n.390, p 204.

Amendment to mean that 'neither a state nor the Federal Government can, openly or secretly, participate in the affairs of any religious organizations or groups, and vice-versa.'[398] According to him, 'in the words of Jefferson, the clause against establishment of religion by law was intended to erect a wall of separation between Church and State ... This wall of separation must be kept high and impregnable. We could not approve the slighted breach.'[399] As a result, the courts began to interpret the establishment clause as prohibiting such things as prayers in public schools, the display of nativity scene at public buildings; the financial assistance to religious schools; the display of the Ten Commandments at schools and court houses; and so forth.

In *Everson* Justice Black claimed that the First Amendment applies to every state and local government. He ruled, in language that is not found in the text of the constitution, that the establishment clause erected 'a wall of separation between church and state.' In support to this argument, Black pointed to the history of revolutionary Virginia, which had suspended the collection of taxes that supported the Anglican establishment in June 1776. 'This court has previously recognized', he contended, 'that the provisions of the First Amendment, in the drafting and adoption of which Madison and Jefferson played such leading roles, had the same objective and were intended to provide the same protection against governmental intrusion on religious liberty as the Virginia statute. ... In the words of Thomas Jefferson, the clause against establishment of religion by law was intended to erect 'a wall of separation between Church and State'. Thus he concluded: 'That wall must be kept high and

---

[398] 330 U.S. 1 (1947).
[399] 330 U.S. 1 (1947).

impregnable. We could not approve the slightest breach'.[400]

Justice Black's opinion demonstrates a remarkable display of historical ignorance or disregard for the drafter's intent. First, the First Amendment says nothing about the establishment of religion by the American states. The first Congress actually rejected a proposal that addressed the question of state-established religion.[401] Furthermore, as Justice Rutledge (who was joined by justices Frankfurter, Jackson and Burton) stated in his dissent: 'Neither so high no impregnable today as yesterday is the wall raised between church and state by Virginia's great statute of religious freedom and the Frist Amendment'.[402]

The original purpose of the First Amendment was to ensure that Congress, that is, the federal legislative, neither introduces legislation that establishes a national religion, nor does it interfere in the religious policy of the individual states – including Massachusetts, Connecticut and New Hampshire – which retained their colonial religious establishments for several decades after the First Amendment was ratified. As for the alleged 'leading role' ascribed to the author of the 'wall of separation' metaphor, Thomas Jefferson played no role in both the draft and the adoption of the First Amendment. He was not even a member of the first Congress that created the amendment and sent that together with all the remaining nine amendments to the American states for their ratification. Neither was Jefferson a member of the Virginia General Assembly that voted to ratify the American Constitution in his native state. Therefore, as Justice Rehnquist argued in his dissent in *Wallace*

---

[400] 330 U.S. 1 (1947), 18
[401] Gutzman, above n.345, p 177.
[402] 330 U.S. 1 (1947), 29

v Jaffree (1985),

> It is impossible to build sound constitutional doctrine upon a mistaken understanding of constitutional history, expressly freighted with Jefferson's misleading metaphor for nearly forty years. Thomas Jefferson was of course in France at the time the constitutional Amendments known as the Bill of Rights were passed by Congress and ratified by the States. His letter to the Danbury Baptist Association was a short note of courtesy, written fourteen years after the Amendments were passed by Congress. It would seem to any detached observer as a less than ideal source of contemporary history to the meaning of the Religion Clauses of the First Amendment.[403]

To base a broad interpretation of the establishment clause on single personal letter written fifteen years after the constitution was ratified is utterly undesirable. One needs first to elevate what was intended to be a personal letter to the same level of a founding document. Then one needs to distort the meaning of that letter insofar as the author is *refusing* to denounce the establishment of religion by the American states.[404] When stating that he contemplated 'with sovereign reverence that act of the whole American people which declared that their legislature would 'make no law respecting an establishment of religion, or prohibiting the free exercise thereof' – thus building 'a wall of separation between Church and State', Jefferson was

---

[403] *Wallace v Jaffree* (1985) 472 U.S. 38, 92.
[404] Justice Black may have had darker motives to distort that letter. He had been a member of the Ku Klux Klan in the 1920s, when the Klan was deeply concerned about the growing influence of Catholicism in the United States. According to Hugo Black Jr., his father 'suspected the Catholic Church... He thought the Pope and the bishops had too much power and property. He resented the fact that rental property owned by the Church was not taxed'; Mark R. Levin, *Men In Black: How the Supreme Court is Destroying America* (2005) 43, quoting Hugo Black, Jr., *My Father* (1975) 104.

refusing to take up the cause of eradicating the American states' establishment of religion. As Patrick Hynes points out:

> The whole American people' is a clever, Jeffersonian way of saying I'm not interested in your parochial problem. Instead, Jefferson stated that it was the constitutional policy of federal government never to establish religion, exactly as other Founders... contended.[405]

The real meaning of that letter lies primarily in Jefferson's reaffirmation of the right reserved to the American states to establish, if willing to do so, their own official religions. Even so, Jefferson had no intention to prohibit Congress from sometimes seeing it fit or desirable to endorse the prevailing religious sentiments of the American people. After all, the First Amendment prohibits the federal government from countenancing or subsidizing the practice of religion. Jefferson would be the first to accept that this amendment is no more than an anti-establishment clause that forbids Congress to *establish* of a national religion, whereas the second half of the guarantee refers solely to the determination that Congress is forbidden to interfere with the practice of religion. Of course, Jefferson is the very Founder who wrote in the Declaration of Independence, with editorial held from John Adams and Benjamin Franklin, 'that all men are endowed their Creator with certain unalienable rights.'

Ever since *Everson*, however, judicial interpretations of the First Amendment often run contrary to the plain meaning of the constitutional guarantee. Building on *Everson* is the notorious 1962 case *of Engel v Vitale* where the Supreme Court maintained the unconstitutionality of a New York policy requiring school

---

[405] Hynes, above n.249, p 40.

districts to have children recite a non-sectarian prayer each morning, which said: 'Almighty God, we acknowledge our dependence upon Thee, and we beg Thy blessings upon us, our parents, our teachers, and our country.' The parents of ten students in the New Hyde Park school district challenged the practice as violating the Establishment Clause. Justice Black, writing for a seven-justice majority, stated: 'There can be no doubt that New York's state prayer program officially establishes the religious believers embodied in the Regents' prayer.'

In *Engel* the court relied on the incorporation doctrine rather than in the original meaning of the establishment clause. To rule that the clause should be applied to the American states, Justice Black's opinion for the majority was rooted in a misunderstanding of the First Amendment's history. Justice Stewart, in arguing that a school initiated prayer does not constitute an establishment of religion, reminded the majority that the Supreme Court itself begins each day invoking the protection of God, and that both Senate and the House of Representatives being their daily sections with prayer. He also noted that U.S. Presidents ask the protection and help of God in their inaugural oath as well as annually proclaim a day of pray, the official U.S. national anthem contains religious verses, the Pledge of Allegiance refers to God, and the American dollar bills contain the words 'IN GOD WE TRUST'. He concluded: 'Countless similar examples could be listed, but there is no need to belabor the obvious. It was all summed up by this Court just ten years ago in a single sentence: "We are a religious people who institutions presuppose a Supreme Being".[406]

If Thomas Jefferson thought there was really no problem in making a direct reference to God as the creator of inalienable rights in the nation's foundational document, why then would he be offended by a New Hyde Park prayer?[407] In reality Jefferson was not insensitive to religion. As President of the United States, he couldn't afford not making a direct reference to God in his annual messages to Congress. Conversely, to forbid the American people to hold prayers in public schools is a flagrant violation of their constitutional rights. Since all that the establishment clause asks is that Congress be prohibited from favouring any religious sect over another, 'it certainly did not inhibit Congress from identifying itself with the religious impulse as such or from authorizing religious practices where all could agree on their desirability.'[408]

In response to *Engel*, in 1981 the Alabama state legislature introduced a statute authorizing a period of silence 'for meditation or voluntary prayer.' Hoping to make the new legislation more acceptable in the eyes of the federal courts, the legislators left out the state-mandated prayer that was held invalid in *Engel*. At trial, in the federal district court, Judge Hand dismissed the plaintiff's claims against Alabama's statute, correctly concluding that 'the Establishment Clause of the First Amendment to the United States Constitution does not prohibit the state from establishing a religion.' Judge Hand

---

[406] *Engel v Vitale*, 370 U.S. 421 (1962), 442. See also: Russell L. Weaver, 'The Establishment Clause of the United States Constitution', *in* P. Radan, D. Meyerson and R. Croucher, *Law and Religion: God, The State and the Common Law* (London: Routledge, 2005), p 43-5.

[407] Gutzman, above n.347, p 179.

[408] Johnson, above n.15, p 209.

argued that the Establishment Clause did not bar Alabama from establishing religion. Clearly, he argued, the clause had been created partly to prevent the federal government precisely from interfering with the states' establishments. Unfortunately, the Circuit Court of Appeal reversed the decision and the case found itself in the U.S. Supreme Court. Relying on its own previous rulings, Justice Stevens ruled for the majority that the Alabama legislation was 'unconstitutional' since it was inconsistent with court precedent, not the Constitution.[409]

An interesting element in that case lays in Justice Rehnquist's compelling dissent. 'It is impossible', He stated, 'to build sound constitutional doctrine upon a mistaken understanding of constitutional history, but unfortunately the Establishment Clause has been expressly freighted with Jefferson's misleading ['wall of separation'] metaphor for nearly forty years.' After noting that Jefferson played no role in writing or ratifying the Establishment Clause, Rehnquist went on to observe that Jefferson 'would seem to any detached observer as a less than ideal source of contemporary history as to the meaning of the Religion Clauses of the First Amendment'. Rehnquist also referred to how the First Amendment was interpreted by the members of the first Congress, noting that James Madison's original draft stated: 'The civil rights of none shall be abridged on account of religious belief or worship, nor shall any national religion be established, nor shall the full and equal rights of conscience by in any manner, or on any pretext, infringed.' When another congressman proposed changing this to 'No religion shall be established by law, nor shall the equal rights of conscience be infringed', he was met with strong criticism

---

[409] *Wallace v Jaffree* (1985) 472 U.S. 38, 92.

and the objection from his own peers who feared very much that this could unexpectedly 'abolish religion altogether in the public sphere, and his proposal was rejected.'[410]

Unfortunately, the court's excessive reliance on Justice Black's reasoning has never been reversed. In *Everson* the modern court began its construction of an 'impregnable wall of separation' between state and religion. The subsequent overzealous application by state and local officials of court rulings became representative of further secularisation and hostility towards traditional religious expressions, a hostility that spread beyond the courts and it now permeates the official public square. Concomitant to this, in 1971 the Supreme Court announced the 'Lemon Test' as criteria for judging state laws concerning to religion. This test came from *Lemon v Kurtzman* (1971), a case in which the state of Pennsylvania was barred from reimbursing non-public schools – mostly Catholic parochial schools – for some of their educational expenses. The program was held unconstitutional. In so doing, the court enunciated the Lemon test that has proved impossible to apply. In order to pass the Establishment Clause muster, the statute in question must meed three criteria: 'First, the statute must have a secular legislative purpose; second, it is principal or primary effect must be one that neither advance not inhibits religion; finally, the statute must not foster 'an excessive entanglement of religion.''[411]

The Establishment Clause by its terms forbids the imposition of an official religion, not statements of religious

---

[410] Gutzman, above n.347, p 183.
[411] Carter, above n.212, p 110.

belief in the course of public dialogue.[412] A majority of the Supreme Court missed this point in *Edwards v Aguillard* (1987), with the suggestion that a law requiring schools to teach scientific creationism is unconstitutional simply because most of its supporters might be religiously motivated.[413] Louisiana's 'Balanced Treatment for Creation-Science and Evolution-Science in Public School Instruction' Act (Creationism Act) forbade the teaching of the theory of evolution in public schools unless accompanied by instruction in creation science. No school was required to teach evolution or creation science. If either were taught, then the other side of the debate should also be taught. Accordingly, the Act was a balanced approach since it allowed that schools could opt to not teach on origins at all. However, if they chose to teach one view of origins, it demanded that the other view should be presented in a balanced way as well. The question was whether this violated the establishment clause of the First Amendment. Regrettably, the Supreme Court, relying on the 'Lemon test', decided by 7-2 that the legislation violated the establishment clause 'because it lacks a clear secular purpose.'[414]

By deciding that the religious convictions of its proponents constitute enough reason to render legislation invalid, the court in *Edwards* misappropriated and misapplied the Lemon test for constitutionality. The test is not an appropriate tool of interpretation particularly in the way it was applied. As Justice Antonin Scalia correctly stated in his penetrating dissent, such a test rests on a 'questionable premise that legislation can be invalidated under the Establishment Clause on the basis of its

---

[412] Ibid, p 112.
[413] Ibid, p 111.
[414] *Edwards v Aguillard*, 482 U.S. 578 (1987), at 585-594.

motivation alone.'[415] Considering the decision in *Edwards*, one may ironically ask whether, as is often the case, 'a teacher's views on evolution grown out of a general belief in materialism – a conviction that physical stuff is all there is, that things come about with no supernatural help, that when we die we die, and so on – should also not be a violation of the establishment clause of the Constitution.'[416]Conversely, if public schools can teach stand-alone theories about creation and human development that are consistent with philosophical materialism, why not to also allow the teaching of theories that are consistent with theological assumptions.[417]As Professor Carter points out,

> A ruling holding that the religious convictions of the proponents are enough to render a statute constitutionally suspect represents a sweeping rejection of the deepest beliefs of millions of Americans, who are being told, in effect, that their views do not matter. In a nation that prides itself on cherishing religious freedom, it would be something of a puzzle to conclude that the Establishment Clause means that a Communist or a Republican may try to have his or her world view reflected in the nation's law, but a religionist can not. Although some critics fear we are already at that point, the truth is that ... we are heading in the wrong direction in our jurisprudence, and if the courts continue to read Lemon as they have, the Establishment Clause might well end up not anti-establishment but anti-religion.[418]

Everson, Engel, Lemon, Edwards, as well as numerous others,

---

[415] See also: Normal Geisler, *Creation in the Courts: Eighty Years of Conflict in the Classroom and the Courtroom* (Wheaton/ IL: Crossway Books, 2007), pp 205-211.
[416] Michael W McConnell, John H Garvey, Thomas C Berg, *Religion and the Constitution*,(New York/NY: Aspen & Business, 2002) p 900.
[417] Ibid.
[418] Carter, above n. 212, p 113.

remain the precedents that the federal courts follow in lieu of the United States Constitution. Based on this line of cases, the courts have undermined religious freedom as well as their nation's Judeo-Christian foundations by declaring the invalidity of long-standing religious practices and expressions. By imputing a non-historic meaning to the phrase 'establishment of religion', the unelected lawyers who comprise the federal judicial elite in the United States have, among other things,

- banned the centuries-old tradition of having invocations at school commencement ceremonies;[419]

- declared unconstitutional for an historical memorial to contain a cross as part of its display (and no matter how many previous decades the memorial had been standing);[420]

- declared unconstitutional for the Ten Commandments to be displayed in a solitary setting at public courthouse and government buildings (despite the fact that the Ten Commandments are depicted in multiple locations throughout the U.S. Supreme Court);[421]

- declared unconstitutional for a nativity scene to be displayed on public property (unless surrounded by sufficient secular displays to prevent it from appearing religious);[422]

---

[419] *Lee v Weisman* 505 U.S. 577 (1992)
[420] *Carpenter v. City and County of San Francisco*, 93 F.3d 627 (9th Cir. 1996); *Separation of Church and State Committee v. City of Eugene*, 93 F.3d 617 (9th Cir. 1996); *Paulson v. City of San Diego*, 294 F.3d 1124 (9th Cir.2002); *Buono v. Norton*, 212 F. Supp. 2d. 1202 (C.D. Cal. 2002), *aff'd*, 371 F.3d 543 (9th Cir. 1994).
[421] *ACLU of Tennessee v. Hamilton County*, 202 F. Supp. 2d 757 (E.D Tenn.2002); *Glassroth v. Moore*, 335 F.3d 1282 (11th Cir.2003); *Adland v. Russ*, 307 F.3d 471 (6th Cir. 2003); *ACLU of Ohio v. Ashbrook*, 375 F.3d 484 (6th Cir. 2004).
[422] *Doe v. Santa Fe Independent School District*, No. G-95-176 (S.D. Tex. May 5, 1995); *Rubin v. City of Burbank*, 124 Cal. Rptr. 2d 869 (Cal. Ct. App. 2002); *Wyne V. Town of Great Falls*, 376 F.3d 292 (4th Cir. 2004); *Turner v. City Council*, No. 306-CV-23 (E.D. Va Aug 3, 2006).

- declared unconstitutional for a city seal to depict any religious element, even if religion is actually the primary influence in the city's founding;[423]
- struck down science curricula they dislike;[424]
- negate a Texas statute exempting religious publication from taxation;[425] and
- struck down a Massachusetts law banning the sale of alcoholic beverages within five hundred feet of a church or school if the church or school objected.[426]

These decisions violate the original meaning of the First Amendment and, in so being, violate the constitutional rights of the American people. We may observe in passing that this abuse of judicial process is not uncommon amongst radical organizations that oppose the presence of religious values or symbols in the public sphere. As one has stated, 'when they cannot stop a bill from being passed by the Legislature and approved by the Executive, or when they find in the statutes laws they do not like, the next recourse is usually the courts.'[427] By contrast, when Founders like Thomas Jefferson, John Marshall and Patrick Henry studied law, 'common-law study was in its nature historical and theoretical. Familiarity with the history of England was essential to it.'[428] As Michael P Schutt points out,

> The study of law was reserved for the person of virtue and character because the law was a subject of dignity and import. Moral reality – distinguishing between right and

---

[423] *Robinson v. City of Edmond*, 68 F.3d 1226 (10th Cir. 1995); *ACLU of Ohio v. City of Stow*, 29 F. Supp. 2d 845 (N.D. Ohio 1998); *Webb v. City of Republic*, 55 F. Supp. 2d 994 (W.D. Mo. 1999).
[424] *Edwards v Aguillard* 483 U.S. 578 (1987).
[425] *Texas Monthly, Inc v Bullock* 489 U.S. 1(1989)
[426] *Larkin v Grendel's Den* 459 U.S. 116 (1982)
[427] McKean, above n.346, p 129.
[428] Gutzman, above n.347, p 173.

wrong, conserving natural rights and duties – is central to its very nature. That is why the student was expected to study Scripture, philosophy, writings on human nature, rhetoric, and ethics.[429]

Now, law students are subject to the case method of interpretation that has transformed legal teaching into a 'science' in which the empirical material of the law is no longer the written text itself, but 'judge-made law', including the more controversial decisions of activist judges. The creator of the case method, Christopher Columbus Langdell, was Dean of Harvard Law School from 1870 to 1895. For him, the study of law should not rest on objective moral standards or the impartial interpretation of the law but primarily in the detached study of precedent. Ever since textbooks on American constitutional law tend to be nothing but collections of judicial opinions, with no historical context and a remarkable disregard for the legislative purpose. As Kevin Gutzman points out:

> If the judges make a particular false assertion about the Constitution in numerous cases, students reading those opinions have no way of recognizing that assertion's falsity. They are provided no tools for analyzing judges' claims – only with scads of the opinions incorporating those claims.[430]

Once American judges aspired to be faithful upholders of the U.S. Constitution. Now they often reflect the spirit of the age and the "cultural revolution" that has transformed western societies. Part of this revolution rests on the premise that freedom can be separated from a higher moral duty and tied solely to personal self-esteem. Such moral relativism has been

---

[429] Schutt, above n.153, p 26.
[430] Ibid.

judicially legitimised in a series of judgments, which has led the U.S. Supreme Court even to redefine the meaning of freedom and of human nature. In the 1992 *Planned Parenthood* case, Justice Kennedy notoriously stated: 'At the heart of liberty is the right to define one's own concept of existence, of meaning, of the universe and of the mystery of human life.'

There is no claim to self-evident moral truths in that statement. The final outcome is a legal system devoid of moral truths; each person being granted autonomy to decide his or her own moral truths.[431]Such a statement is akin to establishing a 'new covenant' for the American people: 'We will be your court and you will be our people.'[432] The People have a 'right' to decide for themselves what is right and wrong, provided, of course, it is generally accepted that there is no higher authority 'in heaven and on earth' than the judges of the Supreme Court.

As beings capable of some sense of right and wrong, the American people should at least be expected to know the unreasonableness of demanding, as part of their freedom or rights, things that do objectively injure others and even themselves. In contrast to the prevailing jurisprudential approach, Hadley Arkes reminds that '[t]he founders began by rejecting scepticism or relativism, in philosophy and morality, and the modern judges, the products of the best law schools in the land, affirm the right of a person to make up his own version of the universe'.[433]

The American judiciary needs to become more aware again of the notion of 'inalienable right', a right we are not competent

---

[431] Paul Kelly, 'Blessed be the egoistic individuals', *The Australian*, July 8, 2017.
[432] Quoted in Charles Colson and Nancy Pearcey, *How Now Shall We Live?* (Wheaton/IL: Tyndale House, 1999), p. 409.
[433] Arkes, above n.229, p 43

to waive or violate even in relation to ourselves.[434] Otherwise, if the unelected lawyers serving at the Supreme Court set out to enforce their misleading doctrines that are plainly at variance with both the intention of the drafter and the literal meaning of words revealed, then one might ask why any such doctrine should not be challenged. America's judges operating the world's oldest justiciable bill of rights can and do regularly strike down laws that have been passed by Congress and signed by the President. As such, majoritarian democracy is judicially curtailed, and in some ways much more so there than in many other countries.

But the problem is that the judicial inroads into representative democracy have dramatically increased in the past few decades. Because such a trend is getting worse and visibly more arbitrary, some constitutional limitations must be re-established as a matter of urgency. As law professor James Allan puts it: 'In the case of the United States the decline in democracy is overwhelmingly being driven by the judges and how they are going about interpreting domestic legal texts, using approaches whose effect is to reduce (sometimes to vanishing point) the external constraints on what they can do and decide'.[435]

Above all, it should always be the case to remind the judicial elite in the United States that it is the text of the written constitution, and not judicial opinion, what ultimately binds in constitutional law. The late Justice Felix Frankfurter of the U.S. Supreme Court correctly reminded: 'Stare decisis is a principle of policy and not a mechanical formula of adherence to the

---

[434] Ibid., p 44.
[435] James Allan, *Democracy in Decline: Steps in the Wrong Direction* (Ballarat/ Vic: Connor Court, 2014), p 20.

latest decision. The ultimate touchstone of constitutionality is the Constitution itself and not what we [i.e., the court] have said about it.'[436] That being so, bad court rulings should be immediately overruled, as a matter of urgency and out of respect for the letter and spirit of the U.S. Constitution. As a celebrated judge of the Australian High Court, Sir Isaac Isaacs, declared:

> A prior decision does not constitute the law, but is only a judicial declaration as to what the law is ... [I]f we find the law to be plainly in conflict with what our predecessors erroneously thought it to be, we have ... no right to choose between giving effect to the law, and maintaining an incorrect interpretation. It is not better ... that the Court should be persistently wrong than it should be ultimately be right.[437]

---

[436] *Helvering vs Hallock* 309 U.S. 16 (1940), 119. (Frankfurter J)
[437] *Australian Agricultural Co v Federated Engine-Drivers and Firemen's Association of Australia* (1913) 17 CLR 261, 275-8 (Isaacs J)

22

Christianity and the American Civil Rights Movement

Stanley Baldwin, three times British Prime Minister between 1923 and 1937, stated in 1934: 'If freedom has to be abolished and room has to be made for the slave state, Christianity must go because slavery and Christianity cannot live together'.[438]

Endorsed by the ancient Greeks and Romans as a common practice, slavery was brought to an end in the West only after people realised the heinous practice is incompatible with Christian morality. Jordan Peterson, a psychology professor at Toronto University, comments:

> The Bible is [...] the foundational document of Western civilization (of Western values, Western morality and Western conceptions of good and evil) [...] The society produced by Christianity was far less barbaric than the pagan – even the Roman – ones it replaced. Christian society at least recognised that feeding slaves to ravenous lions for the entertainment of the populace was wrong, even if many barbaric practices still existed. It objected to infanticide, to prostitution, and to the principle that might means right. It insisted that women were as valuable as men [...] It demanded that even a society's enemies be

---

[438] Nick Spencer, *The Evolution of the West: How Christianity Has Shaped Our Values* (London/UK: SPCK, 2016), p 35.

regarded as human. Finally, it separated church from state, so that all-too-human emperors could no longer claim the veneration due to gods'.[439]

Before the modern world came into fruition, the idea of personal freedom was first nurtured by medieval theologians who theorised on the nature of equality and individual rights in accordance with biblical teaching. The medieval rulers were in many cases advised in the legal codes elaborated by clergymen, normally bishops or monks, who imported into positive law the idea of fundamental rights for human beings as individuals rather than merely members of particular families. Then, later in the seventeenth-century Christian thinkers such as the deeply influential John Locke rested his entire political philosophy on the egalitarian axioms of those theologians who advocated the doctrine of inalienable rights and liberties for every human being regardless of gender, colour or religion. According to sociology professor Rodney Stark of Baylor University,

> As with Rome and all other contemporary civilizations, slavery existed everywhere in early medieval Europe. But among all major faiths, Christianity was unique in evolving moral opposition to slavery, and in about the seventh century, serious religious opposition to it began. By the tenth century slavery had disappeared in most of the West, lingering only at the frontiers. That centuries later slavery was reinstituted in Europe's New World colonies is a separate matter, although here too it was Christianity that produced and sustained the abolition movements.[440]

---

[439] Quoted from Mark Powell, 'Jordan Peterson's Psycho-Religious Heresy', *The Spectator Australia*, 1 February 2018, at https://www.spectator.com. au/2018/02/jordan-peterson-psycho-religious-heresy/

[440] Rodney Stark, *The Victory of Reason: How Christianity Led to Freedom, Capitalism, and Western Success*, (New York/NY: Random House, 2005) p xiv.

The biblical revelation of the character of God is one of the central elements of political and indeed constitutional development in Western civilisation. The Book of Genesis begins with what was the most radical statement in favour of human rights to enter the world. It was that God created all human beings in his own image and likeness. That is the origins of the concept of human rights and dignity in the Western legal tradition. Ancient Greece and Rome did not embody the value of equality of human rights and dignity. In 'democratic' Athens, human rights applied only to a small minority of men in the ruling elite and the franchise never went beyond 10 per cent of the people. Women, slaves and foreigners had no rights at all. And people were not even conceived of as individuals but as members of families.[441] Hence, in *The Victory of Reason: How Christianity Led to Freedom, Capitalism, and Western Success*, Stark explains that 'while the classical world did provide examples democracy, these were not rooted in any general assumptions concerning equality beyond an equality of the elite.'[442] He goes on to state that

> [e]ven when they were ruled by elected bodies, the various Greek city-states and Rome were sustained by huge numbers of slaves. And just as it was Christianity that eliminated the institution of slavery inherited from Greece and Rome, so too does Western democracy owe its essential intellectual origins and legitimacy to Christian ideals, not to any Greco-Roman legacy. It all began in the New Testament.[443]

---

[441] Greg Sheridan, 'Is God Dead? The West Has Much to Lose in Banishing Christianity', *The Australian*, August 26, 2017.
[442] Ibid. p 76.
[443] Ibid.

The idea of equality before the law is an ideal of legality supported by the New Testament. In Acts 10:34, God is declared to be 'no respecter of persons'. Furthermore, Galatians 3:28 states that 'there can be neither Jew nor Greek, there can be neither bond nor free, there can be no male and female, for ye all are one in Christ Jesus.'[444] Statements like these had an undeniable impact on the development of modern democracy and human rights. Professor Berman credits these Christian beliefs as having 'an ameliorating effect on the position of women and slaves and the protection of the poor and helpless' in Germanic law between the sixth and eleventh centuries.[445]

Natural inequality, or the perceived natural superiority of the few over the many, were basic assumptions in the ancient world. Even a celebrated philosopher such as Aristotle viewed slavery as basically inevitable: 'Some are free men, and others slaves by nature', he said. For this reason, Sir Larry Siedentop, in *Inventing the Individual: The Origins of Western Liberalism*, stated: 'Through its emphasis on human equality, the New Testament stands out against the thrust of the ancient world, with its dominant assumptions of "natural" inequality. Indeed, the atmosphere of the New Testament is one of exhilarating detachment from the unthinking constraints of inherited social rules'.[446] According to Sanford Lakoff, who is Emeritus Professor of Political Theory at the University of California, San Diego:

> The Christian teaching with the greatest implications for democracy is the belief that because humanity is created in the image of God, all human beings are of equal worth

---

[444] Eidsmoe, above n.224, p 101.
[445] Berman, above n.295, p 65.
[446] Larry Siedentop, *Inventing the Individual: The Origins of Western Liberalism* (Allen Lane, 2014) p 353.

in the sight of God. Along with the Greek Stoic belief in equality as a reflection of the universal capacity for reason, this belief shaped an emerging democratic consciousness, as Alexis de Tocqueville noted when he observed in the introduction to his study of democracy in America that Christianity, which has declared all men equal in the sight of God, cannot hesitate to acknowledge all citizens equal before the law.[447]

The Bible unambiguously declares: 'It is for freedom that Christ has set us free. Stand firm, then, and do not let yourselves be burdened again by a yoke of slavery'. That so being, '[t]here can be neither Jew nor Greek, there can be neither bond nor free, there can be no male and female: for ye all are one free person in Christ Jesus', concludes the Apostle Paul in his apostolic letter to the Galatians.[448]

Secular critics have none the less dismissed these remarkable biblical statements, arguing that they would have no impact whatsoever on the advancement of human rights and freedoms. Some feminist scholars have even gone so far as to say that rampant sexism continued to be the rule in the early Christian communities. But nothing could be more departed from the truth. To the contrary, these biblical statements had an undeniable impact on the development of human rights and in the West.

Arguably, in an ideal Christian community, all barriers of prejudice must be broken, including xenophobic nationalism (Greek or Jew), religious intolerance (circumcised or uncircumcised), racism (barbarian or civilized), social

---

[447] Sanford Lakoff, *Democracy: History, Theory and Practice* (Boulder/CO, Westview Press, 1996), p 90.
[448] Galatians 3:28

discrimination (bound or free), and last but not least, gender discrimination (male or female). As a result, in the words of Professor Stark: 'Objective evidence leaves no doubt that early Christian women did enjoy far greater equality with men than did their pagan and Jewish counterparts'.[449] As Stark also explains, 'there is virtual consensus among historians of the early church as well as biblical scholars that women held positions of honor and authority within early Christianity'.[450]

The idea of preciousness and equal worth of every human life are primarily Christian concepts. Christians generally believe that each human being has inherent worth by virtue of being created in the image and likeness of God. This idea of inherent human worth is what gave rise to the view that every person is born equal yet with an especially individual purpose. After all, 'the balance between equality and individuality was set in Scripture. Equality of opportunity (as we know it), is necessary to manifest our unique God-given talents'.[451] As noted by Kevin Donnelly, 'concepts such as free will, the sanctity of life and a commitment to the common good are very much influenced

---

[449] Rodney Stark, *The Triumph of Christianity* (New York/NY: HarperOne, 2011), p 124. From its early days, Christian women were involved in numerous church-leadership activities. Women deacons assisted in liturgical functions and administered the charitable activities of the Church. This is in line with Paul's commendation of 'our sister Phoebe' to the Roman congregation, stating that she was a 'deaconess of the church of Cenchrea.' In 1 Timothy 3:11, Paul again refers to women in the role of deacons. In Corinthians 11:11-12, the apostle talks about the right of women to prophesy and that they are as essential as men in Christian fellowship. 'For it is through women that man comes to be, and God is the source of all,' Paul stated. That women would no longer serve as deacons in the late church only reflects the human dictates of a particular tradition, not biblical truth and the reality of the early Christian communities.

[450] Ibid., p 109.

[451] Jennifer Oriel, 'Faithless Australians May Lose More Than Just God', *The Australian*, July 3, 2017.

by the New Testament. The admonition "Thou shalt love thy neighbour as thyself", while not always adhered to, underpins civility, tolerance and respect for others'.[452]

These biblical teachings were particularly relevant during the struggle against slavery in the eighteenth and nineteenth centuries. In England, the leading opponents of slavery were invariably evangelical Christians who had come to the view that since Adam and Eve were the first humans, then they were also the ancestors of black humans — 'are not Adam and Eve parents of us all?'[453] Motivated by such beliefs. William Wilberforce (1759–1833) regarded slavery as a gross violation of God's law.[454] Wilberforce was only 25 years old when he first served in Parliament, in 1780.[455] Over many years he repeatedly introduced a private anti-slavery trade bill in the House of Commons, until the bill was finally passed just two days before he died. Largely as a result of Wilberforce's tireless efforts the British Empire was the first modern nation in the world to outlaw slavery.[456] As sociology professor Alvin J. Schmidt

---

[452] Kevin Donnelly, 'Let's Not Deny Our Christian Roots', *The Australian*, June 15, 2017.

[453] L Staley, 'Review of David M Levi's How the Dismal Science Got Its Name (2001)' in C Berg, J Roskam and A Kemp (eds), *100 Great Books of Liberty: The Essential Introduction to the Greatest Idea of Western Civilisation* (Melbourne/Vic: Connor Court), p 145. 'Christianity is the generative principle of the free world', says Jennifer Oriel. By contrast, as she points out, 'It is no coincidence that at the time of Christianity's decline in the West, Islamists have stepped into the breach to denounce democracy, the secular state and freedom of speech. For all its pretensions to moral authority the PC left is remarkably slow to realise that the foundation of the free world rest on a Judeo-Christian value system. But perhaps that it is too optimistic. It is evident that neo-Marxists on both sides of politics simply don't care'. – Oriel, above n.451.

[454] Charles J Antieau, *The Higher Laws: Origins of Modern Constitutional Law* (Buffalo/NY: William S Hein & Co, 1994) p 81.

[455] William Wilberforce, *Greatest Works* (Orlando/FL: Bridge-Logos, 2007) p 14.

[456] Schmidt, above n.206, p 278.

points out,

> It is difficult to find a better example than Wilberforce to
> show the powerful effect the teachings and spirit of Christ
> have had in fighting the social sin of slavery. No proponent
> of abolition of slavery even accomplished more. Largely
> as a result of his indefatigable efforts, slavery came to a
> complete end in all of the British Empire's possessions
> by 1840, making it the first modern country to outlaw
> slavery.[457]

Unfortunately, slavery was still an important socio-economic institution in the southern region of the United States. To make it worse, in 1857 the U.S. Supreme Court held in the notorious *Dred Scott* case that Congress had no power to outlaw slavery in the federal territories. The court reached its appalling decision by explicitly rejecting the Christian tradition of natural law, and thus appealing instead to a positivistic, or literalistic reading of the Fifth Amendment's prohibition on depriving anyone of property without due process of law. The prohibition was construed as meaning that no federal statute could remove the purported right of slave-owners to take their 'property' with them to wherever they decided to go. For Congress to declare that a person's 'property' could not be taken into a territory without losing it, Justice Taney remarked, 'could hardly be dignified with the name of due process.'[458]

Dred Scott is widely accepted as one of the worst decisions ever made by the U.S. Supreme Court. It is often credited with accelerating the American Civil War by seeking to raise racial apartheid to the level of constitutional principle. In reaching such a notorious decision Justice Taney contended that no

---

[457] Ibid.
[458] *Dred Scott v Sandford*, 60 US (19 How) 393, 407 (1857).

higher law, or inalienable right, should possibility be invoked to prevent a person from having the legal 'right' to retain his or her property, including if this were actually a right to property over another fellow human being: 'There is no law of nations standing between the People of the United States and their Government, and interfering with their relation to each other', Justice Taney said.[459]

But the reality is quite simple: Justice Taney was completely wrong. After all, the early days of American Federation were characterised by the regular evocation of natural law doctrines to provide, among other things, the meaning of 'due process of law' in the Fifth Amendment.[460] In this context, the great Virginian jurist, St George Tucker (who was responsible for the celebrated 1803 American edition of Blackstone's *Commentaries*) wrote in respect of natural law that 'no man nor set of men can have any natural, or inherent right, to rule over the rest.'[461] As noted by Steve Presser:

> At the time of the framing of the Constitution, and shortly thereafter ... the natural law and law of nations foundations for the United States Constitution ... were quite clear to contemporaries. Indeed, property itself was thought to be a concept that derived, ultimately, from natural law ... At the time of the framing of the Constitution the intellectual and spiritual leader of the Southern States, if not of the nation itself, was Virginia. Even in that state, in the late eighteenth century, there had developed a slavery jurisprudence that circumscribed the harshest applications of slavery doctrines through adherence to the basic natural law principle of a

---

[459] Ibid.
[460] Antieau, above n.453, p 81.
[461] Ibid, pp 81–2.

presumption against slavery and in favor of human liberty. Thus, in several important opinions, Virginia slave holders' wishes to manumit their slaves in their wills were implemented, even though at the time the testators died such manumission was not permitted by statute.[462]

Above all, it is important to remind that the fight against slavery in the United States relied almost entirely on a Christian tradition of natural law and natural rights. For instance, free blacks who agitated for the emancipation of their fellow blacks regularly invoked the powerful narrative of liberation in the Book of Exodus, in which Moses leads the captive Israelites to freedom out of the bondage of Egypt. As emeritus law professor Charles Antieau of Georgetown University points out,

> Attacks of the Abolitionists in America were often based upon the theory of natural rights. Horace Mann, speaking in the United States House of Representatives, said: 'The institution of slavery is against natural rights ... an invasion of the rights of man'. Senator William Henry Seward said on the floor of the United States Senate that all men have 'natural rights and inalienable liberty' which forbids slavery. On another occasion, Seward added that 'slavery is contrary to the Law of Nature which is the Law of God'. Charles Elliot, in his 1851 book, 'The Sinfulness of American Slavery', written for the Methodist Church, asserted that man's 'natural liberty' made slavery illegal. The following year, William Hosmer in his book on 'The Higher Law' stated that slavery was contrary to 'natural justice', which he identified with 'the Law of Nature, which is the Law of God'. Gerrit Smith (1797–1874), an active reformer of the century, was a force in the Anti-Slavery Society from 1835 until slavery was abolished. In

---

[462] Steve B Presser, *Recapturing the Constitution: Race, Religion, and Abortion Reconsidered* (Regnery Publishing, Washington/DC, 1994), p 132.

a letter to Henry Clay, he wrote that slavery was opposed to 'the laws of my nature and my nature's God'. Another abolitionist, William Goodell, editor of the anti-slavery periodical, 'The Friend of Man', used both natural right and natural law arguments in support of his crusade against slavery.[463]

Taney's interpretative approach was antagonistic to the American tradition of natural law, and natural rights. Such an approach was heavily influenced by the 'spirit of the age'. The nineteenth century was marked by a period of 'hibernation' for natural-law theory. With the advent of legal positivism (and scientific naturalism) initiated an aggressive reaction against all metaphysics.[464] Indeed, the leading and most influential legal positivist of the twentieth century, Hans Kelsen, explained that the 'changeover of legal science from natural law to positivism went hand in hand with the progress of empirical natural sciences and with a critical analysis of religious ideology.'[465] As a result, no law was assumed to contain absolute or universal value. Rather, all laws were assumed to remain 'subject to historical change and that as positive law it is a temporally and spatially conditioned phenomenon.'[466]

This reality deeply affected even the United States, a nation firmly founded upon natural law philosophy. Until the second half of the nineteenth century, American jurisprudence was primarily dominated by the belief in inalienable rights of the individual, as well as the application of 'self-evident' principles

---

[463] Antieau, Charles J., *The Higher Laws: Origins of Modern Constitutional Law* (Buffalo/NY: William S Hein & Co, 1994), p 81.
[464] Ibid, p 333.
[465] Hans Kelsen, 'The Pure Theory of Law — Part 1' (1934) 50 *Law Quarterly Review* 517, Section II.
[466] Ibid.

of natural law philosophy. However, particularly after the deadly Civil War in the 1860s, American lawyers started to abandon their reliance on the natural law (and natural rights), which had so much guided and inspired just the American Founders but also the earlier generations of American lawyers, including leading American jurists such as John Marshall (1755–1835)[467] and Joseph Story (1779–1845).[468]

Ever since the second half of the nineteenth century, American judges have acquired a tendency to approach the isolated individual as the morally relative measure — and measurer — of all things. Ultimately, 'whether a right receives constitutional designation as a fundamental right depends upon the worldview through which a judge or lawmaker views the Constitution.'[469] Viewed through such a perspective, 'individuals determine whether liberty exists based on circumstance and personal convenience or autonomy, and — without looking to any objective standard of right or wrong — create law accordingly.'[470] Accordingly, the written constitution is not to be interpreted in light of objective standards, but through the viewpoints or 'evolving preferences' of those

---

[467] John Marshall was the fourth Chief Justice of the US Supreme Court, serving from 4 February 4 1801 until his death in 1835. Although judicial review of legislation on constitutional grounds is advocated by Alexander Hamilton in *The Federalist Paper No 78*, Marshall CJ was the first judge to apply the doctrine to invalidate a federal law, in *Marbury v Madison* (1803).

[468] Joseph Story, the first Dane Professor of Law at Harvard University and Associate Justice of the US Supreme Court, linked the natural law to the rights of conscience, which 'are given by God, and cannot be encroached upon by human authority, without a criminal disobedience of the precepts of natural, as well as revealed religion' – Story, above n.162, p 1399.

[469] William Wagner, 'The Jurisprudential Battle Over the Character of a nation: Understanding the Emerging Threats to Unalienable Liberty in America' in Suri Ratnapala and Gabriel A Moens (ed.), *Jurisprudence of Liberty* (Sydney/NSW: LexisNexis Butterworths,2011), p 302.

[470] Ibid, p 300.

attaining positions of power.[471] The final result is described by William Wagner, as follows:

> Contending their special training in the law deems them worthy of actively manipulating the meaning of the Constitution, judges gaze into jurisprudential penumbras to subjectively fashion fundamental liberty interests they personally believe require judicial protection from politically accountable expressions of the people's will (eg, the right to contraception, abortion, etc). Proponents of this approach opine that unelected judges are entitled to personally evaluate whether evolving societal customs justify the judge deeming an interest implicitly in the concept of ordered liberty. When the judge concludes in the affirmative, the judge judicially anoints the interest with 'fundamental' status. With no objective moral standard as a measure, law and liberty become whatever a judge wants them to be in any given situation, or any given day.[472]

Be it as it may, the primary postulation of the Declaration of Independence is that our most fundamental rights are inalienable. Being inalienable, these rights are not a concession of the state but they come to us directly from the hands of a benevolent Creator. This view of our inalienable rights was of special relevance during the civil rights movement in the United States, in the 1960s. Leading the fight against racial segregation was the legendary Baptist minister, Dr Martin Luther King Jr (1929–1968), together with his colleagues at the Southern Christian Leadership Conference (SCLC).

When King made a decision to peacefully march on Good Friday, in 1963, a federal judge issued a restraining order on

---

[471] Ibid, p 297.
[472] Ibid, p 305.

behalf of Birmingham City authorities prohibiting it. King refused to comply with the writ and he was arrested as a result. In solitary confinement, on strips of a toilet paper, King explained why it might be lawful to disobey the law. Since he was asking his supporters to respect court decisions that outlawed racial segregation, 'at first glance', King confessed, 'it may seem quite paradoxical for [him] consciously to break laws.' One may reasonably ask, he added, 'How can you advocate breaking some laws and obeying others?' To such a question King then replied:

> The answer lies in the fact that there are two types of laws: just and unjust. One has not only a legal but a moral responsibility to obey just laws. Conversely, one has a moral responsibility to disobey unjust laws. I would agree with St Augustine that an unjust law is no law at all. Now, what is the difference between the two? A just law is a man-made code that squares with the moral law or the law of God. An unjust law is out of harmony with the moral law. To put it in the terms of St Thomas Aquinas, an unjust law is a human law that is not rooted in eternal and natural law.[473]

In his fight against racial discrimination King elaborated on a distinction between the strictly legal and the objectively moral, which eventually allowed him to conclude that a positive law may be on the books, so to speak, but, because it denies basic rights to a sector of the population, such law 'does not square with the law of God, so for reason it is unjust and any law that degrades the human personality is an unjust law.'[474] Indeed,

---

[473] Martin Luther King Jr, *Why We Can't Wait* [1964] (New York/NY: Signet, 1996), pp 84–5.

[474] J M Washington (ed.), *The Essential Writings and Speeches of Martin Luther King Jr.*, (New York/NY: HarperCollins, 1991), p 49

a significant part of King's strategy to further the civil rights of the black community was to challenge laws by measuring them according to natural law or 'the law of God'. In this line of reasoning to disobey an unjust law is to actually uphold the rule of law. As for the objection that the law of the land should, at all costs, be respected, King could then reply:

> And I subject that the individual who disobeys the law, whose conscience tells him it is unjust and who is willing to accept the penalty by staying in jail until that law is altered, is expressing at the moment the very highest respect for the law.[475]

In an effort to reconcile the civil rights movement's commitment to the rule of law with his personal disobedience to laws that segregate and otherwise oppress, King appealed to the formulations of Thomas Aquinas, specifically his fleshing out of the Augustinian distinction between just and unjust laws. Saint Augustine of Hippo (354–430) insisted that theological considerations should not only permeate legal theory but also constitute the only sound foundation of true law and true jurisprudence.[476] In *City of God*, a classic of Christian theology, he writes that a 'law that is unjust is not seen to be law at all.'[477] If a law is enacted that is neither objectively just nor socially desirable, then, Augustine contends, the very distinction between civil government and an gang of criminals for all practical purpose actually disappears. Devoid of justice, Augustine says, a civil government is no better than an evil system of organised banditry. As Augustine pointed out, 'Justice being taken away,

---

[475] Ibid.
[476] See A H Chroust, 'The Fundamental Ideas in St Augustine's Philosophy of Law' (1973) 18 *American Journal of Jurisprudence* 57.
[477] Augustine, *The City of God*, Bk I, Pt V.

then, what are kingdoms but great robberies? For what are robberies themselves, but little kingdoms?'[478]

St Thomas Aquinas is the paradigm Christian natural law theorist and his celebrated work. His work provided a successful integration of Christian theology and Aristotelian philosophy.[479] Heavily inspired by the writings of Augustine, Aquinas believed in the supremacy of the natural law over positive law. 'Once the king is established', Aquinas argued, 'the government of the kingdom must be so arranged that opportunity to tyrannize be removed. At the same time his power should be so tempered that he cannot easily fall into tyranny.'[480] For Aquinas, 'man is bound to obey secular princes in so far as this is required by the order of justice. Wherefore if the prince's authority is not just but usurped, or if he commands what is unjust, his subjects are not bound to obey him, except perhaps accidentally in order to avoid scandal or danger.'[481] Ultimately, Aquinas declared:

> If it is a people's right to provide itself with a king, and if that king tyrannically abuses the royal power, there is no injustice if the community deposes or checks him whom

---

[478] Augustine, Bk IV, Pt IV. The entire passage is rather illuminating: 'Justice being taken away, then, what are kingdoms but great robberies? For what are robberies themselves but little kingdoms? The band itself is made of men; it is ruled by the authority of a prince ...; the booty is divided by the law agreed on. If, by the admittance of abandoned men, this evil increases to such a degree that it holds places, fixes abodes, takes possession of cities and peoples, it assumes the more plainly the name of kingdom, because the reality is now manifestly conferred on it, not by the removal of covetousness, but by the addition of impunity. Indeed, that was an apt and true reply which was given to Alexander the Great by a pirate who had been seized. For when that king had asked the man what he meant by keeping hostile possession of the sea, he answered with bold pride, 'What you mean by seizing the whole earth; but because I do it with a petty ship, I am called a robber, while you who do it with a great fleet are styled emperor'.'
[479] Chroust, above n.476, p 23.
[480] Aquinas, *De Regimine Principum*, Bk I, Ch 2, p 41.
[481] Aquinas, *Summa Theologica*, II, II, Q 104, art 6.

200

they have raised to the kingship, nor can it be charged with a breach of faith for abandoning a tyrant, even if the people had previously bound themselves to him in perpetuity; because, by not faithfully conducting himself in government as the royal office demands, he has brought it on himself if his subjects renounce their bargain with him.[482]

In this sense, Aquinas's theory comprised a rights-based natural law theory of limited government under the rule of law. The political principles supported by him — the supremacy of the legislature over the judiciary, the independence of the judiciary from political pressure, and the dependence of the judiciary upon previously given legal norms — constitute 'the

---

[482] Aquinas, above note 478, Bk 1, Ch 6. Inspired by Aquinas's words, Pope John XXIII affirms in *Pacem in Terris*(1963): 'Since the right to command is required by the moral order and has its source in God, it follows that, if civil authorities pass laws or command anything opposed to the moral order and consequently contrary to the will of God, neither the laws made nor the authorizations granted can be binding on the consciences of the citizens, since God has more right to be obeyed than men' (para 51). On the Protestant side, the great Scottish Calvinist John Knox (1513–1572) stated that to rebel against an evil ruler is like rebelling against the devil himself, 'who is the one abusing from the sword and authority of God' (John Knox, *On Rebellion* , Cambridge University Press, Cambridge, 1994, p 192). If the political authority rebels against God by violating his eternal laws, Knox declared, 'God hath commanded no obedience, but rather He hath approved, yea, and greatly rewarded, all those who have opposed themselves to their ungodly commandments and blind rage' (ibid, p 95). The Protestant doctrine of lawful resistance against political tyranny was further elaborated by Samuel Rutherford (1600–1661), another Scottish Presbyterian like Knox. In answer to those who relied on Chapter 13 of St Paul's Letter to the Romans, to condemn any resistance against the civil ruler as a resistance to God himself, Rutherford boldly proclaimed: 'It is a blasphemy to think or say that when a king is drinking the blood of innocents and wasting the Church of God, that God, if he were personally present, would commit these same acts of tyranny' – Samuel Rutherford, *Lex Rex, or the Law and the Prince* (1644), *The Presbyterian Armoury*, Vol. 3 (1846), p 34.

fundamentals of justice according to law.'[483] That being so, as Charles Rice pointed out, 'Aquinas analysis is a prescription for limited government, providing a rational basis on which to affirm that there are limits to what the state can rightly do. His insistence that the power of the human law be limited implies a 'right' of the person not to be subjected to an unjust law.'[484]

King's argument is straight out of the *Summa Theologica*. As King himself was a Christian minister, the choice of Aquinas seems obvious. From the perspective of social reform, the choice is particularly important because it appealed directly to 'powerful religious sentiment in order to transcend the division in the southern community.'[485] The formula is correspondingly simple: just laws are those that square 'with the moral law or the law of God' and 'uplift human personally' and should be obeyed. One has both a legal and a more reasonability to obey just laws. By contrast, unjust laws, those laws that are 'out of harmony with the moral law', are 'not rooted in eternal law and natural law', and so they degrade human personality and should not be obeyed.[486]

If King had promoted lawless, instead of the natural law tradition of American constitutionalism, in the struggle to address social injustices, his movement would not have attracted such a widespread support of the American society. Instead, King appealed to the natural-law tradition of American constitutionalism, thus demanding 'the recognition that neither

---

[483] Edwin W. Patterson, *Jurisprudence: Men and Ideas of the Law* (Brooklyn/NY: The Foundation Press, 1953), p 350.
[484] Rice, above n.8, p 85.
[485] Ibid.
[486] John Randolph LeBlanc and Carolyn M. Jones Medine, *Ancient and Modern Religion: Negotiating Transitive Spaces and Hybrid Identities* (New York/NY: Palgrave Macmillan, 2012), pp 189-90.

privilege nor oppression is necessarily a question of the colour of one's skin.'[487] Above all, by appealing to the spirit of the American Declaration, as well as the writings of Augustine and Aquinas, King was entirely faithful to the authentic spirit of the American Republic; a fact which enabled him to boldly proclaim that the laws of Southern states were illegal in a deeper or more profound sense: they violated a higher law that is above human law. As King himself pointed out,

> It is time that we stopped out blithe lip service to the guarantees of life, liberty and pursuit of happiness. These fine sentiments are embodied in the Declaration of Independence, but that document was always a declaration of intent rather than of reality. There were slaves when it was written; there were still slaves when it was adopted; and to this day, black Americans have not life, liberty nor the privilege of pursuing happiness, and millions of poor white American are in economic bondage that is scarcely less oppressive.[488]

---

[487] Ibid.
[488] Martin Luther King Jr., *A Testament of Hope: The Essential Writings and Speeches of Martin Luther King Jr.*, (Harper One, 2003), p 43.

23

The Threat of Judicial Activism

In every constitutional democracy there are three branches of government: the legislative, the executive and the judicial. By virtue of the first, the state creates laws and amends or abrogates those that have been already enacted. By the second, the state administers the existing laws and establishes public security by protecting against possible invasions. By the third, the state punishes criminals or determines the legal disputes that arise either between individuals, or between the state and individuals, or between the federal government and a provincial state. Under the constitutional model which the American framers created, the role of judges is to apply the law but not to make law; they are appointed to administer justice according to the law and not to change it or undermine it. As one might say, a judge who dislikes the constraints of the judicial role because it prevents the fulfilment of a specific policy or agenda should 'leave that group, join or start a political party, and seek to enter a legislature'.[489]

It is sometimes argued that judicial activism may be justified if the legislature is uninterested in reforming certain aspects

---

[489] Dyson Heydon, 'Judicial Activism and the Death of the Rule of Law' (Speech delivered at a Quadrant dinner, Sydney, 30 October 2003).

of the law when the existing rules appear defective. There is a tendency today to suggest that those charged with interpreting the constitution should do so in such a manner as to produce results that accord with the prevailing notions of the day, as if it were the duty of judges to resolve controversial matters that are in reality political-ideological conflicts. If so, the goal would be to liberate these judges from the constraints of the legal method so that their personal values can be imposed on the rest of us. The final result, however, might be the abnegation of law and gradual replacement of the rule of judges for the rule of law. According to the late nineteenth century American constitutionalist, Thomas M Cooley:

> The property or justice or policy of legislation, within the limits of the Constitution, is exclusively for the legislative department to determine; and the moment a court ventures to substitute its own judgement for that of the legislature, it passes beyond its legitimate authority, and enters a field where it would be impossible to set limits to its interference, except as should be prescribed in its own discretion.[490]

Take for instance the recent ruling in *Obergefell v Hodges* ('*Obergefell*')[491] –the Supreme Court same-sex marriage case. The majority's basic premise was that the right to personal choice is inherent to the concept of individual liberty.[492] To be frank, the majority at least acknowledged that 'the Constitution contemplates that democracy is the appropriate process for change, so long as that process does not abridge fundamental rights'.[493] But, it went on to postulate, in rather relativist, or

---

[490] Thomas Cooley, *The General Principles of Constitutional Law in the United States of America* (Little, Brown and Co, 1898) p 158.
[491] 566 US _ (2015).
[492] 566 US _ (2015) 13 (majority opinion).
[493] Ibid 24 (majority opinion).

post-modernist fashion, that fundamental rights somehow evolve and 'come not from ancient sources alone. They rise, too, from a better informed understanding of how constitutional imperatives define a liberty that remains urgent in our era'.[494]

The majority thus candidly concludes that constitutional rights must evolve (according to such post-modern interpretations of the 'living constitution').[495] As such judges stated, '[t]he dynamic of our constitutional system is that individuals need not await legislative action before asserting a fundamental right'.[496] Hence they concluded that same-sex couples should not be deprived of a 'fundamental right' to marry because such a right is apparently inherent to the liberty of the person under the Due Process and Equal Protection Clauses of the Fourteenth Amendment.[497] In his dissent, Chief Justice John Roberts simply reminded that 'a State's decision to maintain the meaning of marriage that has persisted in every culture throughout human history' can hardly be considered a violation of fundamental right.[498]

The American Founders viewed fundamental rights as pre-existing to the formation of the first civil government. In the founding era, it was generally believed that fundamental rights are God-given, 'existing separate and apart from any human grant of power and authority'.[499] Accordingly, fundamental rights are the rights individuals possess 'independent of those

---

[494] Ibid 18-19 (majority opinion).
[495] See, ibid 24 (majority opinion).
[496] Ibid (majority opinion).
[497] Ibid 22 (majority opinion).
[498] Ibid 2 (Roberts CJ, dissenting).
[499] Lael Daniel Weinberger, 'Enforcing the Bill of Rights in the United States', in S Ratnapala and G A Moens, *Jurisprudence of Liberty* (2nd ed, LexisNexis, 2011), p 105.

they are granted by government and by which the justice or property of governmental commands are to be judged'.[500] In the minds of the American Founders, Suzanna Sherry writes:

> Fundamental rights were God-given, and were rights 'which no creature can *give*, or hath a right to take away'. They were, in the language of the Declaration of Independence 'inalienable'. Legislators could no more rewrite these laws of nature than they could the laws of physics.[501]

Based on such an argument, enacting a Bill of Rights was merely to acknowledge God-given rights already in existence. These rights were deemed God-given and more important than any 'right' imposed by the state that certainly ought not to be inconsistent with them. Ratified in 1791, the first ten amendments to the U.S. Constitution resulted from the arguments and influence of George Mason, not Jefferson.[502]He was a Virginia politician and a delegate to the Constitutional Convention of 1787, and one of only three delegates who actually refused to sign the Constitution until a Bill of Rights should be included. Thus Mason made the enactment of a declaration of rights his own 'personal crusade', advocating for the full recognition of fundamental rights that arose from the principles of natural law assumed to be the birthrights of every free individual. According to Russell Kirk:

> Those rights were ... anchored deep in English common law and in the history of the American colonies. Nor did

[500] Randy E. Barnett, *Restoring the Lost Constitution* (New Jersen/NJ: Princeton University Press, 2004) p 54.
[501] Suzanna Sherry, 'The Founders' Unwritten Constitution' (1987) 54 *University of Chicago Law Review* 1127, p 1132, quoting Silas Downer, *A Discourse at the Dedication of the Tree of Liberty* (1786).
[502] Kirk, above n.56, p 77

George Mason think of rights as commandments that the federal judiciary would thrust upon unwilling states and communities. He had from the first a deep uneasiness with the federal judiciary, fearing that federal judges would overrule state judges (which, of course, has come to pass, even to an extreme degree. He would have been astounded that the majority of the Supreme Court of the United States should conjure up a constitutional 'right of privacy' not mentioned even in statute, and deduce from that conjectural right the further right of mothers to slay their progeny in the womb.[503]

This is why Robert P. George of Princeton University, describes natural law as 'a higher law, albeit a law that is in principle accessible to human reason and not dependent on (though entirely compatible with and, indeed, illuminated by) divine revelation'.[504] Such a concept, according to him, is central to the American tradition of unalienable rights, morality, politics, and law. To reject it is tantamount to assuming that all human right is conceived by the state; an assumption vehemently denied by all the American Founders, since it dangerously assumes that what is legally right can be determined by political rulers and the courts of various jurisdictions. By contrast, Professor George appeals to the opening words of the *Declaration of Independence*, which he describes as 'foundational' for our understanding of sources of human rights and liberties.[505] Colson and Pearcey explain how Professor George has been able to teach his law students at Princeton about this undeniable truth in America's

---

[503] Ibid., p 75.
[504] Robert P. George, 'Natural Law Ethics', *in* P L Quinn and C Taliaferro (eds), *A Companion to Philosophy of Religions*, (Oxford: Wiley-Blackwell, 1997) p 453.
[505] Robert P. George, *A Preserving Grace: Protestants, Catholics, and Natural Law* (Grand Rapids/MI: Eerdmans Pubishing,1997) p 94.

constitutional history:

> Professor Robert George of Princeton University made the
> point in a colorful way in civil-liberties course by reading
> to his students the opening words of the Declaration of
> Independence: "We hold these truths to be self-evident,
> that all men are created equal, that they are endowed by
> their Creator with certain unalienable rights". Then he
> looked at the sea of students in the packed lecture hall and
> said: "These are the foundational words of the American
> doctrine of civil liberties, and in light of the content of that
> doctrine as expressed in the Declaration, perhaps it wouldn't
> be inappropriate to begin our deliberations by offering
> thanksgiving to the Creator who endowed us with these
> rights. So let us in silence, each according to his own tradition
> and his own way, give thanks to the Creator for our precious
> rights and liberties". And then he added, … "Those of you
> who are not believers might take this opportunity to reflect
> in silence upon the source of our most important rights and
> liberties, which I believe you too cherish".[506]

Although the 'liberty' under the due process clause protect
only the rights which are 'deeply rooted in this Nation's history
and tradition',[507] in *Obergefell* the U.S. Supreme Court felt
entitled to redefine so-called 'out-dated' notions of rights and
liberty which are found in the *Declaration of Independence*. In his
dissent, Chief Roberts asserted that '[t]he majority's decision is
an act of will, not legal judgement. The right it announces has

---

[506] Colson and Pearcey, above n.433, pp 400-1
[507] *Obergefell v Hodges*, 566 US _ (2015) 2 (Alito J, dissenting). See also, Roberts
CJ, dissenting (at 22): 'The purpose of insisting that implied fundamental
rights have roots in the history and tradition of our people is to ensure that
when unelected judges strike down democratically enacted laws, they do
so based on something more than their own beliefs. The Court today not
only overlooks out country's entire history and tradition but actively re-
pudiates it … [T]o blind yourself to history is both prideful and unwise'.

no basis in the Constitution or this Court's precedent'.[508] Since this approach offers no objective standard for the expanded latitude of how rights might 'evolve', once it is well-ingrained the swings of the ideological pendulum might allow the judicial elite an opportunity to go in any direction according to personal predilections.[509] By arguing that their special training in the law somehow deems them worthy of expanding the interpretation of 'fundamental rights', the following words of William Wagner should be noted:

> [J]udges gaze into jurisprudential penumbras to subjectively fashion fundamental liberty interests they personally believe require judicial protection from politically accountable expressions of the people's will (eg, the right to contraception, abortion, etc). Proponents of this approach opine that unelected judges are entitled to personally evaluate whether evolving societal customs justify the judge deeming an interest implicit in the concept of ordered liberty. When the judge concludes in the affirmative, the judge judicially anoints the interest with 'fundamental' status.[510]

In his strong dissent Chief Justice Roberts explained that '[e]xpanding a right suddenly and dramatically is likely to require tearing it up from its roots. Even a sincere profession of 'discipline' in identifying fundamental rights ... does not provide a meaningful constraint on a judge, for 'what he is really likely to be 'discovering', whether or not he is fully

---

[508] Ibid 3 (Roberts CJ, dissenting).
[509] Thomas Sowell, *Intellectuals and Society* (New York/NY: Basic Books, 2009) p 167.
[510] William Wagner, 'The Jurisprudential Battle over the Character of a Nation: Understanding the Emerging Threats to Unalienable Liberty in America' *in* Suri Ratnapala and Gabriel A. Moens, *Jurisprudence of Liberty* (2nded, LexisNexis, 2011), p 305.

aware of it, are his own values".[511] Whether a right receives constitutional designation as 'fundamental', this depends now on the personal view of a majority of lawyers sitting on the bench, and how they might decide to 'evolve' the constitution according to the so-called 'changing needs' of society.[512] And yet, as the late Sir Harry Gibbs, a former Chief Justice of the High Court of Australia, pointed out:

> [T]he suggestion that the court should formulate a new rule in the light of contemporary values is open to the objection that there is usually a diversity of opinion as to what those values are ... In any case to regard social attitudes as a source of law tends to undermine confidence in the courts, when it is thought that the judges have based their decision on their own notions rather than on the law, and it also renders the development of the law unpredictable since the values which the court recognises are in effect those in the minds of the judges themselves.[513]

Furthermore, as Robert Bork stated:

> The values a revisionist judge enforces do not, of course, come from the law. If they did, he would not be revising. The question, then, is where such a judge finds the values he implements. Academic theorists try to provide various philosophical apparatuses to give the judge the proper values ... A judge inserting new principles into the Constitution tells us their origin only in a rhetorical, never an analytical, style. There is, however, strong reason to suspect that the judge absorbs those values he writes into law from the social class or elite with which he identifies ... An elite moral or political view may never be able to

---

[511] *Obergefell v Hodges*, 566 US_ (2015) 14–5 (Roberts CJ, dissenting).
[512] Wagner, above n.510, p 302.
[513] Sir Harry Gibbs, 'Judicial Activism and Judicial Restraint' (Paper presented at the Constitutional Law Conference, UNSW, 20 February 2004), p 7.

win an election or command the votes of a majority of a legislature, but it may nonetheless influence judges and gain the force of law in that way. That is the reason judicial activism is extremely popular with certain elites and why they encourage judges to think it the highest aspect of their calling. Legislation is far more likely to reflect majority sentiment while judicial activism is likely to represent an elite minority's sentiment. The judge is free to reflect the 'better' opinion because he needs not to stand for re-election and because he can deflect the majority's anger by claiming merely to have been enforcing the Constitution. Constitutional jurisprudence is mysterious terrain for most people, who have more pressing things to think about. And a very handy fact that is for revisionists.[514]

Take, for example, the usual composition of the Supreme Court, Justice Antonin Scalia pointed out in *Obergefell*:

> [T]his Court ... consists of only nine men and women, all of them successful lawyers who studied at Harvard or Yale Law School. Four of the nine are natives of New York City. ... Not a single South-westerner ... Not a single evangelical Christian (a group that comprises about one quarter of Americans), or even a Protestant of any denomination. The strikingly unrepresentative character of the body voting on today's social upheaval would be irrelevant if they were functioning as judges ... But of course the judges in today's majority ... *say they are not*. And to allow the policy question of same-sex marriage to be considered and resolved by a select, patrician, highly unrepresentative panel of nine is to violate a principle even more fundamental than no taxation without representation: no social transformation without representation.[515]

Naturally, the unrepresentative character of the Supreme

---

[514] Robert H. Bork, *The Tempting of America* (New York/NY: Touchstone, 1991) pp 16–7.
[515] *Obergefell v Hodges*, 566 US_ (2015) 6 (Scalia J, dissenting).

Court would be irrelevant if its judicial members were deciding any matter according to the law. Interpreting the law is the beginning and end of the judicial function. In a constitutional democracy, the courts are forbidden to strike down laws unless they are clearly invalid on constitutional grounds. The courts should not control the legislature when they interpret legislation. The term 'judicial control' is actually misleading since it implies that unelected judges can somehow exert discretionary power over a democratically elected legislature. And yet, unelected judges have no such power; rather,all they have to do is discover from the enactments before them what the lawmaker intended to convey.

The ultimate goal of a democratic government under the law is the protection of fundamental rights of the citizen, and that is precisely why the rules and principles established by the U.S Constitution must be faithfully upheld by the Supreme Court. To do otherwise is to betray the means available for upholding the law and ensuring a full vindication of the citizens' interests. Or, in other words, to reject constitutional first principles amounts to a betrayal of the rule of law as well as a blatant denial of the sovereign will of the American people that simply cannot be sustained or tolerated. After all, if the unelected lawyers serving at the U.S. Supreme Court set out to enforce their misleading doctrines, as those which are plainly at variance with both the intention of the drafter (and the literal meaning of words revealed in the constitution) then one might ask why any such doctrines should not be strongly challenged, and such an error of constitutional interpretation more properly addressed.

Of course, the more general and abstract the language of the law, the more difficult the task of interpretation and so much greater the need for ability and integrity in the judges. However, it is clearly a breach of duty for any judicial officer to express their personal opinion on the merits of policy, except so far as this policy does explicitly violate the written constitution. Judges may deem a specific policy pernicious to society but, if there is no sound constitutional provision preventing the legislature from upholding a different opinion, the courts must accept their different opinion of the people's representatives and enforce the law accordingly.

And if it be suggested that members of the judicial branch 'may overstep their duty, and may, seeking to make themselves not the exponents but the masters of the Constitution, twist and pervert it to suit their own political views', as Lord Bryce stated, 'the answer is that such an exercise of judicial will would rouse the distrust and displeasure of the nation, and might, if persisted in, provoke resistance to the law as laid down by the court, possibly an onslaught upon the court itself'.[516] Precisely for this reason, Chief Justice Roberts commented in *Obergefell*:

> Those who founded our country would not recognize the majority's conception of the judicial role. They after all risked their lives and fortunes for the precious right to govern themselves. They would never have imagined yielding that right on a question of social policy to unaccountable and unelected judges. And they certainly would not have been satisfied by a system of empowering judges to override policy judgment s so long as they do so after 'a quite extensive discussion' … In our democracy, debate about the content of the law is not an exhaustion requirement to be checked off before courts can impose

---

[516] Bryce, above n.317, p 225.

their will.[517]

Above all, it should always be considered that it is the text of the constitution itself, not judicial opinion, what ultimately binds in matters of constitutional law. As the late Justice Felix Frankfurter pointed out, '*stare decisis* is a principle of policy and not a mechanical formula of adherence to the latest decision. The ultimate touchstone of constitutionality is the Constitution itself and not what we [i.e., the Supreme Court] have said about it.' That being so, bad court rulings should be overruled because, 'it is not … better that the Court should be persistently wrong than that it should be ultimately right.'

---

[517] *Obergefell v Hodges*, 566 US _ (2015) 25 (Roberts CJ, dissenting).

24

'By the Providence of Almighty God' – Final Considerations

Whether one subscribes to the Christian faith or not, indisputably Christianity is the religious framework upon which American society was built. Christian morality is the cement of American constitutionalism, and Christian concepts of natural law and natural rights traditionally operate as necessary limitations to human ambitions that all governments possess.[518] Yet it is society itself that must ensure a proper measure of order and justice for all. Arguably, the American order of justice and liberty may not be sustained without the Christian moral framework that Americans have traditionally embraced. As the American Founder James Adams stated, the U.S. Constitution 'was made only for a moral and religious people. It is wholly inadequate to the government of any other'.[519] Or, as Thomas Jefferson asked rhetorically, 'Can the liberties of a nation be thought secure when we have removed their only firm basis, a conviction in the minds of the people that these liberties are of the gift of God?'[520]

---

[518] Ibid., p 30.
[519] John Adams, 'Message from John Adams to the Officers of the First Brigade of the Third Division of the Militia of Massachusetts, October 11, 1798.
[520] Thomas Jefferson, 'Notes on the State of Virginia, Query XVIII: Manners' (1791).

As can be seen, the Founding Fathers of the United States thought that the connection between politics and faith was particularly important for the preservation of public morality and good government. They supported the right of citizens and governments to actively promote Christianity. And they saw education and religion going hand in hand. That is why the first House of Representatives, on the day after it passed the First Amendment, on 24 September 1787, passed also and by a substantial two-to-one majority, a resolution calling for a *National Day of Prayer and Thanksgiving*. Above all, none of the Founders who were the driving force behind the enactment of the American Bill of Rights advocated for anything like a wall of separation between church and state. On the contrary, they thought that each of the American states and localities should encourage Christianity. They agreed among themselves that the new nation should not have an established church, but even at the federal level they supported the hiring of congressional and military chaplains, and requested President Washington to issue a Thanksgiving Proclamation.

Contrary to the approach adopted by today's judicial elite, the American Founders embraced a doctrine of separation of powers because they believed, like Montesquieu, in the biblical idea of corruptibility of human nature. Asserted in Montesquieu's political philosophy (though undeniably confirmed by lessons of history), the doctrine of separation of powers acknowledges that civil authorities are naturally inclined to get corrupt and to abuse their power, in particular when such a power is concentrated in the hands of a person or only a few of them. Hence the Founders reasoned that, in order to secure and protect the United States from tyranny, the power of the state should be divided into several branches of government, so if any particular branch becomes ultimately evil or corrupt, the other branches remain trustworthy and able to check any wayward influence.

Ever since 1947 – when the Supreme Court decided the case of *Everson v Board of Education* – a false doctrine of rigid church-state separation has pushed religious freedom and observance out of public schools and public affairs generally. This long series of highly controversial decisions, beginning in the 1950s – against prayer in public schools, Bible reading, quotation of certain religious passages from public documents, display of the Decalogue on school walls – have exerted a chilling effect on religious freedom in the United States.[521]

Many American judges and politicians maintain an entirely different meaning of the first clause to the First Amendment that was intended by the Founders. They persist in fancying that somehow or other the United States' Constitution speaks of a 'wall of separation' between church and state. Of course, no such a phrase appears in any American legal document. Those words about the hypothetical 'wall', which have provoked so much controversy, occur merely in a letter written in 1802 by Thomas Jefferson, addressed to an assembly of Baptists.[522]

The Constitution of the United States, though not on its face

---

[521] Interestingly enough, as Russell Kirk reminds, 'Formal schooling was commenced by churches. Ultimate questions cannot be answered except by religious doctrines – unless we are prepared to embrace the dialectical materialism of the Marxists. Congress has chaplains and support religious services. Every president of the United States has professed his believe in divine wisdom and goodness. Yet certain judges deny the right of young Americans to pray in the public schools – even as an act of 'commencement' concluding their twelve or thirteen years of school'.– Kirk, above n.56, p 159.
[522] Ibid., p 155.

exhibiting an openly Christian nature, was heavily influenced by the religious experiences of the American Founders. This is no more evident than in the First Amendment, which guarantees (among other things) religious freedom and tolerance, thus prohibiting an established national church so as to limit the power of the federal government. Since the Founders recognized that it would be impossible to agree upon a single Christian denomination to be established at a national level by the federal government (and many feared giving the national government power in this area), there was almost a complete agreement that if there was going to be an establishment of religion, it then should be made at the state or local level.[523]

When American judges have turned to the Founding period to shine light on the meaning of the religion clauses, they have overwhelmingly relied on an ahistorical approach based on the personal views of Thomas Jefferson. Such an approach is unreliable because Jefferson was not even involved in the drafting (and ratifying of) the First Amendment.[524] Because of such an approach, however, Christianity is becoming a 'Forbidden Faith' insofar as public policy and legislation are concerned, although there is far more indulgence of 'non-western' religions as parts of advancing so-called 'multiculturalism' and 'global education'.[525] Of course, the original concept of 'church-state separation' was not really intended to create freedom *from* religion. Rather, the original intent was to establish freedom *for* religion against undue governmental intervention, and freedom

---

[523] See: Daniel L. Dreisbach, 'In Search of a Christian Commonwealth: An Examination of Selected Nineteenth-Century Commentaries on References to God and the Christian Religion in the United States Constitution' (1996) 48 *Baylor Law Review* 927-1000.
[524] Ibid.
[525] Kirk, above n.56, 159.

for Christianity in particular.

America is not an ethnic group or an ethnically homogeneous nation. Instead, the United States was founded as a quintessentially Christian nation. One of the primary beliefs upheld by the first colonizers is the statement found in the Declaration of Independence that humans are born equal and endowed by their Creator with certain unalienable rights. Accordingly, the first purpose of every government is to protect these unalienable rights, which are particularly our God-given rights to life, liberty and property. For this to become a reality, however, the Founders understood the crucial role of Christianity as foundational to both the formation and preservation of the United States as a free and democratic nation organised under a representative government that is effectively under the law.

Edmund Burke wrote in his seminal *Reflections on the Revolution in France*: 'The effect of liberty to individuals is, that they may do what they please: We ought to see what it will please them to do, before we risque congratulations, which may soon be turned into complaints'.[526] Over the past forty years or so, it seems that Americans have ceased to become more aware of their national history, including the nation's founding Judeo-Christian values and beliefs. Americans today tend to talk a great deal about 'sustainable growth' and 'environmental conservation', but they pay very little or no attention to the notion of sustainable freedom, and the legal conservation of individual rights.

---

[526] Edmund Burke, *Reflections on the Revolution in France* (New York/NW: Penguin Classics, 1982), p 91.

But sustainable freedom requires reasonable levels of order and restraint, and the only restraint that does not contradict freedom is actually self-restraint. Unfortunately, self-restraint is the very thing the indulgent form of freedom that is so pervasive today seeks to obliterate. This, of course, is anything but truly liberating. 'Liberty may be endangered by the abuses of liberty as well as the abuses of power', wrote James Madison in *The Federalist*.[527] In a true democracy, one might say, the government and their subjects are basically one and the same. However, the democratic constitutional framework depends not just on the character of public authorities, but also on the character of the people as a whole. It is really tragic to observe that a considerable parcel of the American people have lost touch with the essential elements that once shaped their great nation. Such a carelessness may prove to be lethal for the preservation of constitutional rights and freedoms.

---

[527] Alexander Hamilton, James Madison and John Jay, *The Federalist* (Middletown/CN: Wesleyan University Press, 1961), p 425.

ABOUT THE AUTHOR

Dr Augusto Zimmermann LLB (Hon.), LLM *cum laude*, PhD (Monash) is an internationally known legal scholar and is broadly recognised as one of Australia's strongest proponents of free speech. He is Professor of Law at Sheridan College in Perth, Western Australia, and Professor of Law (adjunct) at the University of Notre Dame Australia, Sydney campus. In addition, Dr Zimmermann is a former Law Reform Commissioner with the Law Reform Commission of Western Australia (2012-2017) and a former Associate Dean (Research) at Murdoch University's School of Law (2009-2013). Professor Zimmermann is President of the Western Australian Legal Theory Association (WALTA), the Editor-in-Chief of the Western Australian Jurist law journal, an elected Fellow at the International Academy for the Study of the Jurisprudence of the Family (IASJF), and a former Vice-President of the Australasian Society of Legal Philosophy (ASLP). He is a prolific writer and his books include *Western Legal Theory: History Concepts and Perspectives* (LexisNexis, 2013), *Global Perspectives on Subsidiarity* (Springer, 2014, with Michelle Evans), *No Offence Intended: Why 18c is Wrong* (Connor Court, 2016, with Joshua Forrester and Lorraine Finlay), and *Christian Foundations of the Common Law – Volume 1: England* (Connor Court, 2018), etc. In 2012, Professor Zimmermann was awarded the Vice-Chancellor's Award for Excellence in Research at Murdoch University, and also awarded two consecutive Murdoch School of Law Dean's Research Award, in 2010 and 2011. He has been included, together with only twelve other Australian academics and policy experts, in 'Policy Experts' –

the directory of Washington-based The Heritage Foundation for locating knowledgeable authorities and leading policy institutes actively involved in a broad range of public policy issues, both in the U.S. and worldwide.

CPSIA information can be obtained
at www.ICGtesting.com
Printed in the USA
LVHW080759081118
595976LV00012B/170/P